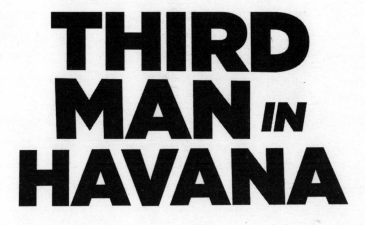

THIRD MAN IN HAVANA

TOM RODWELL

THIRD MAN IN HAVANA

FINDING THE HEART OF CRICKET IN THE WORLD'S MOST UNLIKELY PLACES

WITH MAPS AND ILLUSTRATIONS BY
STEVE DELL

CORINTHIAN BOOKS

Published in the UK in 2012 by
Corinthian Books, an imprint of
Icon Books Ltd, Omnibus Business Centre,
39–41 North Road, London N7 9DP
email: info@iconbooks.co.uk
www.iconbooks.co.uk

Sold in the UK, Europe, South Africa and Asia
by Faber & Faber Ltd, Bloomsbury House,
74–77 Great Russell Street, London WC1B 3DA or their agents

Distributed in the UK, Europe, South Africa and Asia
by TBS Ltd, TBS Distribution Centre, Colchester Road
Frating Green, Colchester CO7 7DW

Published in Australia in 2012
by Allen & Unwin Pty Ltd,
PO Box 8500, 83 Alexander Street,
Crows Nest, NSW 2065

ISBN: 978-1-906850-30-2

CONTENTS

To

Kathleen Rodwell née Goodfellow (1906–2001)

Frank Sutliffe Rodwell (1899–1987)

Suzanne and Fred, for sharing my life and my love of cricket

*And my apologies to Graham Greene (1904–91),
who hated the game.*

ABOUT THE AUTHOR

Born and bred in Leicester, Tom Rodwell is a lifelong advertising man whose love of cricket has led to his working with several cricket charities over the past twenty years. Married with a son, he lives in Hertfordshire, and is now a Visiting Professor at London Metropolitan University's Business School, and Chairman of the Lord's Taverners.

ACKNOWLEDGEMENTS

John Arlott said that above all cricket is 'a human game', and in the end it's the people met on my cricketing journey that make everything worthwhile. From Shabby, my terrible wicket-keeper, to Julien Cahn, who first got me involved in a cricket charity and introduced me to Reg Scarlett at the Haringey Cricket College in London. Mikey Thompson and Tony Joseph were pupils at the college and have been with me most of the way. Huge respect — and love — to those guys, Mikey now back in Jamaica and Tony in Qatar.

Abroad the list is endless, and although it's invidious to isolate particular individuals who've made a difference, the following is a small sample of people who I'm proud to have met along the way: Courtney Walsh, Brian Breese and Jimmy Adams in Jamaica; Leona Forde in Cuba; Liliana Fernandez in Panama; Clifford Hinds and Jeff Thompson in New York; George Sheader and Abu Hamed in Israel; Jayananda Warnaweera and Philippe Duamelle in Sri Lanka; Norman Nyaude in Zimbabwe; Nicholas Muramagi, Simon Ojok and John Nagenda in Uganda; Charles Haba in Rwanda; Elijawa Jacob in Tanzania; Sidney Benka-Coker and Francis Mason in Sierra Leone. All these and many others have achieved far more than I ever could, using their talents, whether cricketing or not, to help solve all sorts of different issues in the countries they love.

Finally, thanks to my editor Ian Marshall for persuading me to write the book, and for shepherding its progress, and special thanks to artist Steve Dell for his wonderful wibbly-wobbly drawings and maps.

FOREWORD

by Courtney Walsh

I consider it a great honour to be asked to pen a few words to introduce Tom's book *Third Man in Havana*. It's an opportunity to say thanks, because it was he and his charity colleagues who helped me to set up The Courtney Walsh Foundation a few years back.

Although the aims of the Foundation sound a bit serious – 'to inspire and empower positive change in Jamaica's disadvantaged young people in order to improve their prospects in education, training and employment' – it's really just about using cricket in different ways to help loads of kids, while having fun at the same time. This is just what Tom's written about in this wonderful book.

The book is set not just in countries where cricket's a passion, like Jamaica, but also where it's much less well-known, such as in Israel and Cuba. Although Cuba is very different from Jamaica, it's not far away, and I've been able to see for myself the interest that there is in cricket in a country that, like Jamaica, is mad about its sport.

It's my privilege, being an ambassador-at-large for Jamaica, to be able to travel the world to help my country. One of those trips was to London, and it was there that I was introduced to tapeball cricket, a basic version of the game that was being played on a basketball court underneath a motorway. Now that's very different from the sort of cricket I played, but I could see that the kids from the area were having a ball, under the watchful eye of their coach Mikey Thompson, who is now head coach of the foundation back in Jamaica, where he grew up.

I was lucky when I was growing up in Jamaica. Being part of a strong family kept me on the straight and narrow. But others aren't so lucky, and if we can get them playing cricket, understanding about fair play, and enjoying themselves in a team, then there's a better chance that they'll become good citizens and, who knows, even play for the West Indies like I did.

Coming to England to play county cricket for all those years opened my eyes to what cricket had to offer, and being able to represent my country, Jamaica, at the same time led to my dream coming true: playing for the West Indies, alongside some of the greatest players in the history of the game. This enabled me to travel to wherever cricket was played, and I was paid for the privilege. But I always tried to remember my roots, to respect my opponents and always to give my best.

But cricket isn't just about what goes on at the top level – it's about having fun, and it can also be about helping make a difference to people's lives. I have seen how cricket has changed the lives of many, whether they be prisoners, the disadvantaged or the disabled. This book tells some wonderfully uplifting stories from all around the world, about how the game has helped such people – always with fun at the heart of that help.

This book makes me feel good about the game I love, and I learned a few things too. I had to laugh about Tom's catch off my bowling in Spanish Town jail, though. Honestly, despite what he says, it was a really easy one!

Remember, if we all help one another we can all have a good time.

One Love,

The Hon. Courtney Walsh, Order of Jamaica,
Ambassador-at-large

INTRODUCTION

This book is the story of what happened when an ordinary cricketer who'd had years of fun playing the game at home and abroad was given the chance to use the game to help young people from around the world. These young people were often suffering from all sorts of disadvantages, but we were able to help them to get to know cricket, have fun playing it and maybe even improve their lives.

It's the story of eighteen trips to twelve countries over a six-year period, from 2005 to 2011; a story of government involvement and intrigue; of cricketing authorities sometimes helping and sometimes hindering; of the struggle to get the projects off the ground; of incredible sights seen; but above all of the amazing people met along the way, people often working in very difficult and dangerous conditions.

Now this all sounds very worthy, but the essence of sport is fun, and this book describes work in some countries where cricket is hardly known, such as Israel, Rwanda and Cuba, as well as others where it's embedded in their culture, such as Jamaica and Sri Lanka. But in all of them the cricket that is played and the young people that are encountered, victims of poverty, war or disability, bear witness to the power of the game to surprise, to entertain, and even to educate.

As all bowlers know, it's sometimes difficult to concentrate on your line and length, but in Israel it's doubly so when a platoon of infantry troops from the Israel Defence

Forces, based at the Erez crossing into the Gaza Strip, has just demounted from an armoured personnel carrier and is on the boundary, both of the cricket pitch and of Israel, shouting and pointing rifles at you, especially when your iffy leg-spin is fragile at the best of times.

My bowling was under pressure in Rwanda too, having to demonstrate to aspiring young Hutu and Tutsi cricketers how to pitch the ball on middle and hit the top of the off stump, in a stadium in Kigali that only a few years previously had been at the centre of their genocidal civil war.

As an inconsistent batsman, being bowled out isn't necessarily the end of the world, but it's doubly disappointing when you're representing your country against Cuba's best, watched by a largely uncomprehending and unlikely crowd, including Ken Livingstone and Lord Moynihan. It's also frankly frightening when the bowler's name is Stalin, and he seems to have inherited all the eponymous Soviet leader's hatred of anyone standing in his path to glory.

My fielding isn't what it was, so normally taking a decent catch from a good shot by an ex-Jamaica batsman off the bowling of West Indian legend Courtney Walsh should be a cause for huge celebration. But not when the victim is a convicted murderer serving life in Jamaica's Spanish Town jail, who'd been looking forward to his first game in years, and I'm the reason he's got out in the first over.

In Sri Lanka its 30-year civil war had only just ended, and ex-Tamil Tiger child soldiers were still being held at the Ambepussa internment camp, despite protests from UNICEF. But the inmates were still able to enjoy their first taste of cricket, even if it was being played behind barbed wire, and despite the fact that they couldn't celebrate sixes hit over the heavily guarded boundary fence.

Before these trips, I'd thought that cricket was just about batting, bowling, fielding and having a good time, but they have taught me that it can be about much more than that. A lot is written about how sport can break down prejudices, transcend boundaries, and bring people together, but much of this comment is so general as to sometimes be almost meaningless. However, these journeys made me appreciate the power of sport, and especially cricket, to deliver a lot more than just plain fun. It really can help make the world a better place, as I hope this book will show.

PART ONE

1

A PASSAGE TO INDIA

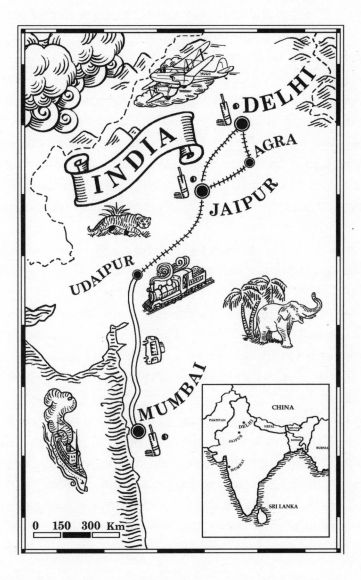

FRANCES EDMONDS, wife of the ex-England player Philippe, wasn't that keen on cricket and wrote a very funny book about England's unsuccessful 1986 tour of the West Indies called *Another Bloody Tour*. Reading the book, one can understand her feelings, but every cricketer loves touring, and while the week-in week-out roster of league or friendly games can become a bit dreary, the tour is always the highlight of the season, and for years I ran a team that did little else.

I worked for an advertising agency that was once described in the press as 'a cricket team which does a bit of advertising'. Well, it was the 1980s when life was easier. Still, I did manage to help launch some decent ad campaigns, such as the Smash Martians, the Sugar Puffs Honey Monster and the Cresta Bear, while mainly worrying about where the next tour should be.

It started off innocently enough with trips to Kent, playing against such teams as Marshside CC, who played at the aptly named Sheep Dip Meadow. Then to Devon and Cornwall, playing against pub teams like The King of Prussia and The Pig's Nose. The Pig's Nose ground overlooked the sea and games were regularly abandoned because of the sea fret, which was no hardship with the pub being so close.

Our big match was always against Tideford CC, whose ground was on a concave slope so extreme that third man's position could only be confirmed by the swirling cigarette smoke above his head, just like in the old Hamlet cigars ad (though that was in a golf bunker). A lot of village clubs are dominated by one family, but Tideford took it to extremes by once fielding an entire team of Snowdons. Funnily enough, they were all very tall too – they could well have been named after the Welsh mountain.

We then ventured over the water to Jersey, where the pitch was in the middle of an airfield and their best fielder had only one arm. Having gone that far, we reached out to those two powerful cricketing nations, Belgium and France. In Belgium, we took on the Royal Brussels Cricket Club. They played at Waterloo, so every game was, of course, 'The Battle of Waterloo', but, unlike in 1815, we normally lost.

France, it must never be forgotten, are the current holders of the Olympic silver medal for cricket (having lost to England at the 1900 games, though it was the only match played) so their is a proud history. In France, our initial opponents were the Standard Athletic Club in Paris, and we always played on the final day of the Tour de France, thus providing a much-needed alternative sporting spectacle to those not smitten by cycling. Then we went to Cabris, in the south of France, where goats had to be moved from the pitch before we began playing. This was often tricky to negotiate with the locals because Cabris is old French for 'goat', and the pesky animal's local significance is of almost religious proportions. Cabris isn't far from Cannes, and one year our wicket-keeper, Shabby, missed the Saturday fixture to pick up an award from the Advertising Film Festival, only to return at the start of the Sunday game still wearing his dinner jacket, which he duly played in, making his wicket-keeping even worse than usual.

Venturing across the Mediterranean to Minorca, we played on a lovely ground in the middle of the island which was infested with wild tortoises. These can easily be mistaken for old cricket balls, and when they are so mistaken it makes them even wilder.

Our confidence growing, we took in Mombasa in Kenya, where proper cricket is played on the wide hard beach, so if the fielding gets too dull you can just step back over the boundary into the cooling sea. One of our players, a large Welsh comedian called Barry Williams did just that, promptly fell asleep in the sea and was hospitalised with sunstroke. Easily his best joke.

Then came Barbados, which was a rugby tour really, but with a game of cricket played the following day. Saturday afternoon rugby injuries and Saturday evening drinking injuries had ravaged the Sunday cricket team, so I had to frantically engage the hotel manager to put a team together. The wages of two waiters were paid to enable them to play, and he then said that there was a good cricketer just coming off the golf course who might like a game. As he approached the bar, I thought he looked a bit past it, but the manager assured me he could still play a bit. It was Sir Garfield Sobers, who joined us for a drink, but said he was too tired to play. He added that if we'd asked him the day before, he would have played. If only …

But a tour of India was the catalyst that transformed my love of the game by helping me see that cricket could be much more than just fun. A London-based Indian cricketing friend of mine, Sunil Amar, an accountant who'd founded the Kensington CC, had been pestering me for years to take a team to India. So in 1985 a team comprising mainly advertising people, but also including a banker, a restaurateur, a journalist and a farmer was assembled for an assault on the subcontinent's best.

While we travelled in cosseted comfort, wore brand new touring cricket kit and wielded the finest equipment money could buy, everywhere we went we saw hundreds of impromptu games being played by both kids and adults dressed in everyday scruffy clothes and using whatever they could find for bats, balls and wickets. The Indian teams we played against were as well equipped as we were, and were oblivious to this contrast, since it was just the norm in India, but as the days went by the nagging unfairness of the gap between rich and poor started to eat into me.

A lot of 'proper' cricket people had lent their support for what was then a very ambitious tour. Kapil Dev wrote the foreword to our tour brochure, saying: 'On behalf of all cricket people in India, I would like to welcome you to our country and to wish you good luck and good fun.' Geoffrey Boycott, having previously played for my team and scored a cautious 99 against a powerful Turville CC XI, also wished us well with a more personalised message: 'My highest individual score in Test cricket was against India in 1967 [246 not out] and in 1981 I pushed a four past midwicket off Dilip Doshi against India to beat Sir Garfield Sobers' Test aggregate of 8,032 runs.' I like Geoffrey and, to be honest, if I'd scored that many runs I'd not keep quiet about it either!

With other good wishes from Phil Edmonds, John Snow and Christopher Martin-Jenkins ringing in our ears, we approached our first game against the hotel staff in Delhi

– the Oberoids – with confidence and, astonishingly, won it with ease. The ground was on the site of the 1857 Indian Mutiny, which obviously held bad vibes for the locals.

This surprising win was not a good move, as word went round that maybe we weren't as bad as we said we were, and the next game against an Indian XI was a different story. They'd picked four current Indian Test players, including Kirti Azad, who had been in India's 1983 World Cup team, and the light blue turbanned spinner Maninder Singh. A large crowd of Indians and vultures had assembled at the Northern Railways ground and they weren't disappointed. The Indian XI struggled to 402 for three off their 40 overs, with Kirti Azad scoring 73 in fifteen minutes before retiring, which got the crowd whooping and hollering. The vultures weren't disappointed either as they spent the entire innings circling around Shabby, who wasn't looking at all well and was keeping appallingly.

Luckily, I'd rested myself for the game, having scored a stylish, winning seventeen the previous day. My place had gone to a drinking mate from my village pub, the Green Dragon, a local farmer called Richard Styles who joined the touring party at two days' notice when he realised that with winter approaching, he had very little to do for the next few months. Who'd be a farmer, eh? At 60 for five we were in trouble, but Farmer Styles took a liking to Maninder Singh's floaty offspin and with a flurry of agricultural swipes ended his innings on 51 not out as part of our respectable total of 191.

Kirti Azad said he'd never seen anyone bat so well against Maninder, and joined us for the uproarious after party. Maninder couldn't make it, still wondering what had gone wrong. Kirti wrote in our scorebook: 'Grand effort and good luck. Have a nice stay. Cheers!' He's now an MP and TV personality. I bet he's good at both.

The next game was in the capital of Rajasthan, the 'Pink City' of Jaipur, a most wonderful place where the Maharajah's old palace, the Rambagh, was the best hotel in town, and luckily ours for the night. One of our team, Ian Sippett, was with his girlfriend and was so taken with the place that he got married there in an interminable Hindu ceremony, despite the fact that neither of them were Hindus. As I write, they're still together, so maybe it wasn't such a mad idea after all.

The previous Maharajah died while playing polo, but the current incumbent, a friend of Sunil's, was more of a cricket man and had challenged us to a game. The ground was astonishingly beautiful, surrounded as it was by encastellated mountains, and certainly before the match 'The Maharajah of Jaipur's XI v BMP' looked good in the scorebook. But there were shades of the Indian XI in Delhi and we were again well beaten, this time by 135 runs, although we did win the beer match, a groundbreaking concept new to our Indian friends. Perhaps it gave them the idea for the IPL. Their skipper was a charming fellow who played for East Grinstead in the summer, and was puzzled as to why we'd come so far to play such poor cricket. Harsh, but fair.

We also managed to squeeze in the sights of Udaipur and Agra in Rajasthan, thankfully avoiding having to play cricket there, before moving on to our final fixture in Bombay, which it was then still called. British colonial pomp was very evident in the Gateway to India, built to celebrate the arrival of George V in 1911 for the Delhi Durbar, and the wonderful Victoria Station, which makes ours look almost suburban.

But the highlight had to be the string of cricket gymkhanas that were laid out in the 19th century behind the majestic sweep of Marine Drive. Mindful of the city's religious diversity, clubs were formed for the local Muslims, Hindus and Parsees, as well as our own splendid Bombay Gymkhana where the locals were sadly not so welcome. These four communities played in regular quadrangular tournaments before the war, and in the late 1930s they were joined by an Anglo-Indian Judeo-Christian team called the Rest. But Gandhi, not a cricket lover, put paid to all this frivolity after the war.

Our match was against the Parsees, descendants of persecuted Persians who sought refuge in India in the sixth century; they had been the pioneers of Indian cricket. Apparently there are now only about 100,000 Parsees left in the world, but that was easily enough for them to generate a team sufficient to inflict another heavy defeat on our motley crew, who by then were suffering from tour fatigue.

As ever, a good crowd had watched our less than impressive performance and many of them were street kids who hung around both teams, enviously eying up the equipment and asking to play with it among themselves. We just couldn't ignore the joy that transformed their dusty faces when they picked up a proper cricket bat and were able to hit a proper cricket ball, perhaps for the first time. We were leaving the following day and after a very quick discussion we decided to donate all of our cricket kit to the locals. Some of it we gave away to the kids who'd been watching, which created pandemonium, and the rest we left to our Parsee friends who knew where it could be distributed to best effect. The germ of the idea to do something more than just play cricket for fun was starting to grow, and a conversation that evening made it blossom.

The tour had been a great success and on our final night in Bombay I spent a lot of time with one particular member of my team, an entrepreneur with a famous cricketing name: Julien Cahn. Julien's grandfather was Sir Julien Cahn, another entrepreneur who made a lot of money before the war in the furniture business, and spent a lot of it on sport: on hunting in the Midlands and on cricket both in the Midlands and around the world. He had been president of both Nottinghamshire and Leicestershire CCCs; indeed, my father knew him after the war in Leicester, although sadly he died soon after. His no-expense-spared cricket tours around the world were so good that apparently an invitation to join Sir Julien Cahn's XI was often regarded as superior to one from the MCC.

Julien had enjoyed this tour, and reckoned his grandfather would have done too, with its emphasis on fun as much as good cricket. It had also given him the idea for a new business – an upmarket Indian restaurant called the Bombay Bicycle Club, inspired by a sign he'd seen above a shop as we ambled through Bombay. Only a few years later, the restaurant was doing so well that a chain was developed and sold for a few million. His grandfather would have been proud.

But what Julien really wanted to talk to me about was the possibility of my helping him with a cricket charity called the London Cricket College, of which he was chairman.

His argument was persuasive. 'Tom,' he said, 'you've had too much fun playing cricket and organising tours, and you've seen the effect merely giving away some cricket kit has had. It's about time you used your meagre talents to help other kids like these, who haven't been so fortunate. Come and work with me at the London Cricket College, you won't regret it.' I did, and I didn't regret it, because this was the catalyst that took me even further round the world, playing cricket, having fun, but this time, doing a bit of good as well.

After we got back to England, I dropped Geoffrey Boycott a note to thank him for his support. He replied: 'Glad you had a super time. The best way to visit India is in short doses and then it's great.' Well, we'd had a short dose in India, and it certainly was great.

2

LONDON – WE ARE
THE WORLD

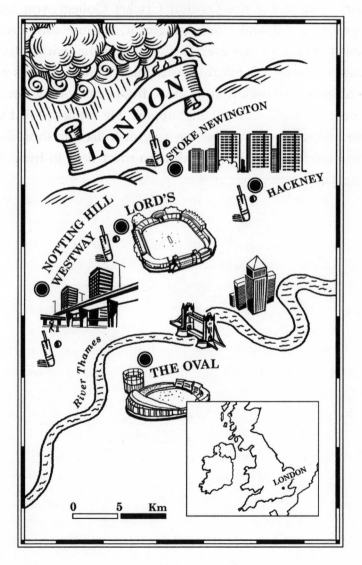

THE LONDON CRICKET COLLEGE was a charity that had been set up a few years previously as the Haringey Cricket College. It was intended to help (mainly) young black and Asian lads achieve their potential in cricket and in life. Its mantra was, 'to produce good cricketers and good citizens'. All charities have to have grand-sounding objectives, otherwise they don't get any income, but this one was sincere.

The college achieved its objectives through a unique combination of adult education and cricket coaching in the unprepossessing surroundings of the Selby Centre, a run-down leisure centre in Haringey, right in the heart of one of London's earliest immigrant West Indian communities.

The charity was run by Reg Scarlett, an imposing Jamaican who'd played a few times for the West Indies in 1960 as an off-spinning all-rounder. Reg had become a big pal of Garry Sobers, but this wasn't enough to stop him soon losing his place to the great Lance Gibbs, so he had come to England to play in the northern leagues. Eventually he settled here happily with his English wife, and decided to share his cricketing knowledge.

There's a good story in Sobers' autobiography about how he scored 150 not out at Lord's in his final Test match in England in 1973, after spending all night out on the town with his old mate Reg Scarlett. *Wisden* states that during this innings Sobers had to retire temporarily with a stomach upset, which shows what kind of a night it had been.

Reg was an old-fashioned disciplinarian – except when Sobers was involved – which naturally a few of his tearaway tower block charges didn't like. However, his methods and his West Indian chutzpah produced a string of talented and

14

successful young black cricketers who went on to play first-class cricket, such as Adrian Rollins and Frank Griffith at Derbyshire, Keith Piper at Warwickshire and Mark Alleyne, who was the youngest player ever to score a century for Gloucestershire, beating Wally Hammond's record, and who is now the MCC head coach.

The effect that the judicious mixture of cricket and education had on some of the students was neatly summed up by Adrian Rollins who said: 'If it hadn't been for the London Cricket College I'd probably now be in prison rather than having a first-class cricket contract.'

Compared to the ramshackle Selby Centre, the college's cricket team was deliberately 'old school', resurrecting as its name London County, the club that W.G. Grace founded as his own county team in 1899. The cricket played was mainly against the first-class counties' second teams, who were regularly beaten, and also on tours to Reg's beloved West Indies. But Reg had to fight hard to get his charges first-class contracts, such was the conservatism in the game at that time. He was helped in this by one of his coaches, the late great Fred Titmus, who was better connected in the upper echelons of the game.

Two of the graduates who didn't warm to Reg's disciplinarian approach were Mikey Thompson and Tony Joseph, neither of whom made it into first-class cricket but who were both to play a huge role in my cricketing travels round the world and in the lives of the hundreds of young people their work touched.

Mikey is a giant of a man, with the build of a heavyweight boxer and the good looks of Samuel L. Jackson, to whom he claimed to be related. He was born in London and brought up peripatetically in Jamaica and in London with his eleven brothers (a cricket team for goodness sake!). He only finally came back to London in his early twenties, so missing out on a first-class cricket career in either Jamaica or England – too young in Jamaica, too old in England – although, as he often reminded me, he was undoubtedly good enough.

Tony Joseph was younger than Mikey, under whose giant wing he was nurtured. A tall, pale-skinned handsome Antiguan, again born in London, he was still connected to his roots, particularly as his cousin was Sir Vivian Richards. While his batting wasn't quite up to Viv's standards, it was stylish and effective and he was also a dangerous medium-pace bowler. His apparent languidness didn't appeal to Reg, but even Mikey had to admit that Tony was a better cricketer than he was.

Even though the first-class game seemed closed to Mikey and Tony, other opportunities opened up. Mikey spent some time playing and coaching in Ireland, where he helped nurture the very early cricket career of Ed Joyce, who went on to play for both Ireland and England, and where as 'the only black man in Dublin' Mikey was a much sought-after companion in the city's uproarious nightclubs. Tony had a more eye-opening secondment, coaching in the townships of Natal in South Africa. Their experiences confirmed to both of them that cricket coaching with a purpose was what they wanted to do.

I was enjoying helping to run the charity, which in turn ran the college, and meeting the sort of people I wouldn't normally have come across. To be honest, I was also revelling somewhat in the reflected glory of the successes of the graduates. But a series of events in 1996 and 1997 changed all that.

At the end of 1996, Reg was headhunted to set up the proposed new West Indies Cricket Academy in Antigua, a great accolade for him, but a problem for the college, which had been his baby. As it happens, the academy was never set up, which might help to explain why West Indies cricket is now so poor. But, more importantly, 1997 produced a 'perfect storm' for the college when the new government immediately cut sports Lottery funding, while the founding of the England and Wales Cricket Board to look after all cricket also affected funding.

So even though we managed to persuade Deryck Murray, the ex-Warwickshire and West Indies wicket-keeper, to take Reg's place, and got some new funding in from the private sector, within a year we had to close down the college, despite it having been described by the then Sports Council as 'the most successful sports academy in the world'.

A sad item from the last set of minutes states: 'As from the 9 September 1997 The London Cricket College will cease trading and seek legal advice on appointing a liquidator'. Such a waste. But it wasn't just us failing. Matthew Engel aptly summed up the situation of England cricket in the 1997 *Wisden* thus: 'Amid the general global mood of cricketing expansion, England is a spectacular and potentially catastrophic exception.'

After such a disappointing experience, I was happy to go back to concentrating on an advertising career and playing cricket for fun. But I'd got the bug of helping other people enjoy the game and learn from it, albeit now in the more salubrious surroundings of Berkhamsted, Hertfordshire, rather than Haringey, London N22.

I kept in touch with Mikey and Tony from time to time, played the odd game of cricket, and sampled the best of Mikey's wife Rose's Jamaican cooking, which he used to bring in a huge hamper to Lord's during the Test matches. My job was just to supply the booze, which was easy. While everyone else in Lord's sacrosanct picnic area was sampling smoked salmon and pork pies, Rose's rice and peas, curry goat and red snapper brought a touch of Sabina Park to St John's Wood, London NW8.

Mikey and Tony had both started work at another cricket charity called the London Community Cricket Association (LCCA), which had been linked to the old London Cricket College. When we met they regaled me with the great work they were doing, but they also said that the charity was always short of money and needed re-energising if it was to survive the new millennium.

The LCCA had been founded in the aftermath of the 1981 Brixton riots to try to get some harmony back onto the streets. It is sad that more than 30 years later possibly even greater problems still exist on the streets of London's inner city, making one wonder whether lessons have really been learned.

In the years following 1981, the LCCA had undertaken cricketing projects in the most difficult areas of London, in rundown housing estates, inner-city schools, special needs schools, prisons, and had even started to spread its wings overseas, but its constant financial problems were becoming an issue, just like at the London Cricket College in 1997.

I was asked to become chairman, which worried me a bit after my disappointing experience at the college, but I said yes because I thought it would be fun working with Mikey and Tony again and that maybe I'd learnt enough to make a success of this challenge. It was indeed fun, and led to projects around the world, but it was also harder work than advertising – although to be honest most is. Effectively I was running a small business with all the responsibilities involved, for no financial gain.

But talking of money, it must never be forgotten that 95 per cent of all cricket in the UK, and around the world, is run by thousands of selfless volunteers, also for no financial gain, so my involvement was nothing out of the ordinary. But as the years rolled by, the work did become very much out of the ordinary.

The people who run small charities, whether paid or unpaid, are generally motivated by the right reasons, but are often naive as to the realities of the world, a bit like some academics, and this can sometimes reduce the impact of the work that they do. The LCCA was no exception to this, so there was a lot of work to be done to try to stabilise the organisation. Thankfully the real work of the charity remained excellent and interesting, which made the job of securing its future much easier.

The creativity of the organisation knew no bounds, and, just like in advertising, all that was needed was to harness that creativity to business and financial reality. Even simple things like a change of name from the worthy London Community Cricket Association to the snappier Cricket for Change had an immediate effect on internal morale and external recognition.

So the work didn't change a great deal, but more financial security and improved relationships with the cricketing establishment enabled more work to be done, as more funds were attracted from a stronger base of partners.

Thus blind cricket – where sound from within a special ball allows the game to be played by blind people – had been played for some years, but was energised when Mikey took over as head coach of the England Blind Cricket team, leading to their winning the first Blind Ashes against Australia in 2004. I watched the vital last match in the series, at Bradfield College, which England won to secure the Ashes with an unbeaten century from the totally blind Tim Guttridge. It was his final match before retirement from the game and he is now quite rightly a member of the MCC.

One of England's opening bowlers that day was a young man who later worked for the charity, adding credibility to the disability programme as he was visually impaired himself. The match took place on the same day as a one-day international at Lord's, and we managed to get a victory message through to *Test Match Special*, so Christopher Martin-Jenkins proudly announced over the airwaves that 'England have won the Ashes' to a somewhat bemused radio audience, before adding that it was the Blind Ashes that had been won, a year before their sighted colleagues emulated their achievement at The Oval.

This was disability sport at the highest level, but when filtered down to cricket in schools that specialise in young people with a disability, self-esteem rises exponentially as they realise that they can take part in sport, too. Tony did a lot of work in these schools and explained to me why cricket seems to work so well with a range of disabilities. The game itself, despite its seemingly complex character, nevertheless has a formulaic structure to it that enables it to be broken down into bite-size chunks that are easily understandable. This is particularly attractive to Down's Syndrome kids, who are able to get into the game more quickly than other sports which might appear less complex on the surface. The simple act of being able to catch a ball can give the empowerment and the self-belief that can change a 'can't-do' attitude to a 'can-do' attitude, and that can start to transform a young person's life.

Other team sports, such as football, are too fluid and too quick for this to happen. In cricket, there's time to get your head around what's going on, thus making the game's 'slowness' a big benefit to young people lacking confidence because of their disability. In cricket, as Tony always says to his pupils 'your time will come', be it stopping a ball, taking a catch, bowling a good ball or hitting a good shot. Interestingly, I think that this is the same dynamic that keeps ordinary cricketers like me going. Even if only one good thing happens in a whole afternoon of cricket, it's enough to keep you interested and to make you turn up next week.

Tony said that the major difference between 'standard' cricket coaching and coaching those with a disability was that in the former you're coaching for excellence, whereas in the latter you're coaching for confidence. Other things around the game help too — even the scoring system. This not only promotes numeracy, but many autistic kids who play love the detail that's generated by all the statistics and quickly become brilliant scorers as well as players.

Getting the team together for an away fixture becomes an incredible adventure. Clambering onto the bus. Checking who's there and who isn't. Is the kit on board? What about the drinks? All these are important little milestones to be achieved and are all part of the harmony that generates 'team spirit', one of the main reasons we all play sport. And then the drive back, 'always a nightmare', said Tony, as the noisy post-mortems take place.

Some of the case histories of lives that have been changed are startling. Bilal had no verbal communication before he started playing cricket, but the game gave him a voice. Ferdie's physical disability had stopped him from playing any sport, but taking up cricket enabled him to demonstrate what he could do at The Oval during the England v India tea interval, in front of 25,000 spectators. Young Ryan even wrote a story about how cricket had transformed him from being 'a nobody into a somebody'. The parents tell the same stories. 'Bethany's just so much happier now she's found your cricket,' said one, and the same parents often become valued volunteers as they've seen how much more confident their own children have become.

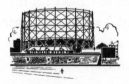

In the inner city the challenges are different, but the results can be just as rewarding. One of the more obvious surprises about inner-city London is that there are hardly any cricket pitches. There are just the two Test grounds at Lord's and The Oval, and three posh grounds at Westminster School,

The Honourable Artillery Company in the City of London and the Guards' cricket ground in Chelsea, all either in great demand or very expensive to hire, or both.

The creative answer to that problem was to play a version of the game that doesn't need flash facilities — tapeball cricket. Tapeball is played widely in the West Indies and in Pakistan, and uses a tennis ball covered in electrical tape to mimic most of the properties of a cricket ball; either a wooden or a plastic bat; anything for stumps; and simplified laws. There is no need for a proper pitch. So, games were organised on all-weather football pitches, basketball courts — anywhere that was flat and available.

At an early demonstration of tapeball in Stoke Newington, the ex-Surrey coach Micky Stewart (father of Alec) watched as Maurice Chambers, now at Essex, bowled to Shaun Levy, who had a spell at Middlesex, and described it as 'chaos cricket'. This was exactly the intention — to strip away the mystique of the game, leaving just the fun and the energy. Most of the players were not up to Maurice and Shaun's level of ability, but that didn't matter, as they were enjoying themselves, keeping out of trouble, and eventually even opening new avenues in their lives.

Some went on to Hackney Community College, getting them back into education, and joined Mikey's Hackney College cricket team, which had picked up some strong fixtures. The rule was that if you'd done all your work, attended all your lectures, and were good enough, you earned the right to play cricket.

The players were a mixture of black, white and Asian kids, mainly in their late teens, a potentially combustible mixture, so Mikey introduced some more rules. Turn up on time.

No fighting. No disrespecting each other. And because a lot of the Asians preferred speaking their own languages, Mikey insisted on only English being spoken to stop any cliques developing. The team was an eclectic bunch. Neneto was a teenager whose father, a policeman in Jamaica, had been murdered. Kenny's family home in Montserrat had been destroyed by the Souffriere volcano, and Irfan had suffered prejudice in India as a religious Muslim but was now introducing cricket to the North London mosque.

Despite these differences and problems, all started to develop quickly into good cricketers and young men determined to make something of themselves, with Neneto and Irfan later going to university and Kenny becoming an excellent coach. The desire for higher education surprised me, and such was the demand that a few years later Mikey and I created a Community Cricket Coaching degree at London Metropolitan University, which in 2010 produced its first graduate, a young black guy who'd once been on Spurs' books now looking forward to a teaching career.

I couldn't get to their first all-day game against the MCC at Chigwell School, where London Cricket College graduate Frankie Griffith was now director of cricket, so I asked Mikey to keep in touch with me as to how the boys were doing. He rang me at about 3pm saying that he was driving the team minibus back down the M11 to London. 'Was it that bad?' I said.

'No,' he answered. 'They batted first [the MCC always do] and were rolled over for ninety-eight, and we knocked them off without losing a wicket, it's like the old days, man.' It was, and I was very proud of him, and the boys. Not for nothing has Mikey been dubbed 'the godfather of inner-city cricket' by *The Voice*, black London's newspaper.

At another match, I got a team of mainly ex-Leicestershire cricketers together to play against the boys. I'd got involved with them through an attempt, unsuccessful as it happened, to improve the County's management, but had stayed in touch. So, Carl Crowe, Neil Burns, Vince Wells and Devon Malcolm together with some good ringers turned up to play in sunny Essex on the hottest day ever recorded (38°C/100°F), 10 August 2005.

We were short, so I played, as well as Mikey and my son Freddie. We were also giving a debut to our new wicket-keeper, a young Vietnamese boy from Shoreditch called Hans. This wouldn't necessarily have been a big story, but Mikey let me bowl a few overs of dodgy legspin off which the aforesaid Hans made a quite brilliant stumping. Mikey and Freddie took wickets too, but they always do, so I hope you'll forgive this particular indulgence. Despite the heat, all the pros were happy to share their cricketing knowledge in the nets with the boys after the game, demonstrating the inherent decency and enthusiasm of most professional cricketers.

Reg Scarlett, on one of his regular visits back to England, had turned up to watch and was pleased with what he saw. In a different guise, we'd managed to recreate some of the ethos of the old London Cricket College, and (surprise, surprise) it was one of his lower-achieving pupils, Mikey who'd done it. 'Well done, Mikey,' he said, 'I knew you had it in you.' Mikey gave him an old-fashioned look, but said nothing and just smiled.

Mikey encouraged the boys to become Level 1 and Level 2 cricket coaches so that they could earn some money and help with events. These 'urban cricket coaches' helped set up 'Take Back the Streets' cricket events in Hackney with Mikey, as an antidote to the all too prevalent gun, knife and drug crime in the area. Their work was supported by the Metropolitan Police, who were keen to encourage all the gangs and gang members to do something more positive with their lives.

These were a good introduction to the game and as results were encouraging (anecdotally, low-level crime diminished in the area), the Met then provided cash to organise year-round cricketing activity on difficult housing estates across London. This resulted in such astonishing matches as young Muslims playing against young Orthodox Jews in Stamford Hill, and 'sworn enemy' postcode gangs playing against each other in Tower Hamlets and Bermondsey.

The highlight of every season was the Inner-city World Cup, which took place at the Indoor School at Lord's, courtesy of the MCC, with teams picked according to their ethnic background. Thus, Kenya, Pakistan, Bangladesh, India, West Indies, Zimbabwe, Sri Lanka and even Afghanistan all played tapeball cricket for the trophy. I know this goes against the received wisdom that we're all Brits together, but just once a year it was fun for everyone to remember their heritage, a bit like the annual Notting Hill Carnival.

One year the Met Police's Special Patrol Group – the one which is armed to the teeth – put in a team to try to build bridges. Even the army took part, looking to demonstrate that they were open to ethnic minority recruits. They played one match against the young Afghan asylum seekers, a tense affair since some of the army team had served in Afghanistan, and a couple of the Afghans were from Helmand province, but thankfully there were no untoward incidents, such was the power of the game to transcend, if for only a few minutes, some of the issues that dominate the world today.

For a laugh, I later introduced the army cricketers to the Barmy Army, and played in a game on the Woolwich Barracks ground between the renamed Army Army team against the Barmy Army team, which amazingly the latter won and which still makes me chuckle.

The Met Police's involvement got stronger and stronger, as they saw the benefits of what we were trying to do. They organised a fancy launch for a new project in the unlikeliest of cricket surroundings, under the Westway, the motorway which tears in and out of West London and splits the stuccoed mansions of South Kensington from North Kensington's tower blocks.

The area witnessed the Notting Hill race riots in the 1950s, Britain's first, but although it's quietened down now, there's still grinding poverty next to oligarchic wealth, which is why a sports centre has been built in the space underneath the roar of the motorway. One of the guys looking after the centre is a cricket-loving old Rasta from Jamaica who occasionally performs with Damon Albarn's cartoon Gorillaz band. He adds to the street cred of the site, meaning that cricket is tolerated in a football-dominated area. There's no classic cricket pitch here, just some basketball courts and an Astroturf football pitch, but plenty of space for a weekly series of tapeball cricket matches to help keep the kids out of trouble.

This particular week was a PR event, so the cameras and the celebs were there to drum up publicity and hopefully money, so that the programme could be continued. The most important thing was that the kids were having a whale of a time. There was a team of young Sikhs from Southall, Bengalis from the East End, and the local tyros, a mixed black and white team from Notting Hill. A team of girls had also showed up, just to prove to the boys that they could do it too.

The Metropolitan Police were there in force, including the Commissioner, a pleasant Lancastrian who didn't look like a copper at all, although he told me he started off on the beat in Manchester. Maybe the soft south had had an effect. He later resigned over the *News of the World* phone-hacking scandal, but that's another story. The police were not there to keep the peace but because they were sponsoring the tournament, having realised that if young kids have something to do in their spare time, then they're less likely to cause trouble. Common sense, really.

Two of the celebs there were ex-West Indies great Courtney Walsh and my old chum Devon Malcolm, who does an awful lot of charity work. Courtney was in London doing some work for the Jamaica Tourist Board and the PR company had persuaded him to come along and join in. Courtney was wearing his tracksuit and looked just as fit as he did in his prime 20 years earlier. He and Mikey went way back in Jamaica, where they played against each other in colts matches, so this was a fun reunion. Devon was born in Jamaica too, but he came over to England when he was a boy.

He still looked good and seemingly had lost none of his pace since he destroyed the cocky South Africans at The Oval with nine for 57 in 1990. 'You guys are history,' he shouted after they'd bounced him out, and he was right.

Playing cricket with both Courtney and Devon was a huge treat for the kids, but both said they were just grateful for what cricket had done for them, and that they were happy to spread the gospel that cricket isn't just for superstars. After a couple of hours the games were over, the speeches were made, the prizes were given out and the photographs were taken, so we did what everyone who calls him or herself a cricketer does at stumps — repaired to the pub to chew over the day.

Courtney was amazed at what he'd seen. He'd seen good cricket being played on a cold November day, under a motorway in inner-city London, and, forgetting the PR hoopla, he'd also seen nothing but smiling black, brown and white faces who'd had a great time, made new friends, and couldn't wait to come back next week. He then shocked us by saying: 'Look, Jamaica's got similar problems to London, and cricket's still a big game, why don't you come across and help me try to set up something there?'

Mikey's eyes immediately lit up. Most years he went back to Jamaica for a few weeks and he'd already set up blind cricket there and done some work in the ghettos, but the chance to help Courtney, one of the greatest cricketers of all time, to set up an organisation like ours in the country where he grew up is one he couldn't pass up. I was just as exhilarated by the prospect myself.

We both answered at the same time: 'Yes'.

3

JAMAICA – 'ONE LOVE'

BOB MARLEY'S 'ONE LOVE' is Jamaica's unofficial national anthem, but that sentiment was soon dispelled as our bus got caught up in a gun battle on the main road from the Montego Bay airport to Ocho Rios, on our way down to Kingston. The scene was more like Marley's song 'Three O'Clock Roadblock' than his signature tune.

So commonplace is gun crime in Jamaica that in the next morning's *Gleaner* the incident warranted only a few lines. No one had been killed. It had just been a case of mistaken identity by the police, which happens a lot apparently.

Mikey then regaled us with the tale of his last brush with gun crime in Jamaica which turned out to be two policemen fighting over a girl who obviously didn't want to share her 'One Love'. And then the bus went past the famous 'Twin Pussy' rock a bit further along the road, which got Mikey going on another altogether different, albeit related, subject ...

It's easy for Brits to think of Jamaica as a succession of Sandals Resorts where the rum is all-inclusive, but in Jamaica, life is all-inclusive. It has the highest per capita concentration of churches in the world and yet the highest murder rate in the world too. So life is cheap but God is everywhere, presumably turning a blind eye.

I'd just read Ian Thomson's book on Jamaica, *The Dead Yard*, which is a sometimes terrifying description of Jamaica and the problems it faces, seen through the eyes of its key players. But the more you get to know Jamaica the better it becomes, and our job is optimism, so despite its problems there is a lot that Jamaica can be proud of.

It is a land of superlatives. The finest coffee in the world comes from the Blue Mountains, which glower over Kingston like big friendly giants. The fastest man in the world is Jamaica's Usain Bolt, and the fastest woman in the world is Jamaica's Shelly-Ann Fraser. Jamaica produced the first great black cricketer, George Headley, whose first-class batting average of 94.93 made the cricket world call him 'the black Bradman'. In Jamaica it's the other way round — Bradman was 'the white Headley'.

In the 1970s another Jamaican Mikey, Mikey Holding, bowled with a 'whispering death', thus stoking the 'Fires of Babylon' in the greatest West Indian team ever. The fast bowler's production line at Jamaica's Melbourne Cricket Club then produced Courtney Walsh, the West Indies' leading wicket-taker of all time, whose concern for all things Jamaican has made him an honorary ambassador for his country. One end of Melbourne Cricket Club is the 'Holding End' and the other is the 'Walsh End' — what a terrifying prospect for any batsman coming to the crease.

It seemed no time at all since we all agreed to come over to help Courtney set up a charity to use cricket to help solve some of the island's problems, but we had been lucky in quickly finding some great partners to make it happen. In this case, British Airways had come up trumps with the flights (thankfully Kate, their PR lady, is a cricket fan), because they were keen to promote their new route from Gatwick to Montego Bay. Their generosity meant posh seats at the front of the plane on our first flight out, where we found ourselves sitting next to Grace Jones, coming back to Jamaica from her home in Paris for a funeral. Although she'd been away from Jamaica for many years she hadn't lost her love of it – Jamaicans rarely do – and was amazed at what we were trying to achieve.

Music and sport are two of the great Jamaican exports and there are huge links between the two, so she knew all about cricket. Her public persona (remember when she attacked Russell Harty on his TV show?) would suggest a difficult diva, but she was nothing like that, just a bright, world-aware lady who's seen a lot of life, good and bad, and wished us well.

Torrance, a good man at the Jamaica Tourist Board, had kindly sorted our hotel, the Pegasus, which although wonderful had sad cricketing memories, because it's where the then Pakistan coach Bob Woolmer died. Our other partner in the programme was none other than HM Government. While crime rates in Jamaica are high, sadly there are also over a thousand Jamaican nationals in English prisons, and there's a big British government programme both to help Jamaica run its prisons well, and also to repatriate Jamaican prisoners from the UK. The theory is that running cricket programmes in Jamaican prisons might ease the rehabilitation of prisoners back into mainstream society and improve the behaviour of those for whom prison will be for life.

There had been some success in the UK with sport in prisons, under the 2nd Chance project, notably in the brand new Ashfield Young Offenders Institution in Bristol, where all sorts of programmes were in place to try to avoid the new prison suffering the same fate as the old one on the same site, which was burned down by the inmates. The new name, 'Ashfield', at least proves that our prison service has a sense of humour.

It always helps that the top end of British government is full of cricket lovers – the Lords and Commons cricket team has a fixture list to die for – and luckily our government outpost in Jamaica, the British High Commission in Kingston, was no exception. After you've got through several layers of security at the gate, the first thing you see in the plush grounds surrounding the colonial classical mansion is a well-used cricket net.

Although a Jamaica posting is not exactly a bed of roses, it can't be all bad if one can sharpen up for the day's work with a quick net session before it gets too hot. A party had been organised for us when we arrived so that we could talk to all the key people. It's amazing the variety of issues that cricket can be seen to help. The Jamaica sports minister and Jimmy Adams, the ex-West Indies captain and proud Jamaican, both wanted to make Jamaican cricket great again by reaching out into the communities. A charity called Rescue Jamaica wanted to get some normal life back into the ghettos, and the people at the Sir John Golding Disability Centre wanted to get cricket onto their sporting curriculum. While all these tasks would be difficult, there doesn't seem to be anything standing in the way of getting started. But the prisons idea was a much more difficult sell, or should it be cell?

We arranged to meet the head of Jamaica's prisons in her office in downtown Kingston the following morning. We needed all the help we could get, so Courtney was there, as well as Brian Breese, who, having been a teacher in England and Jamaica for years, went on to run Jamaica cricket. Brian was a garrulous enthusiastic Welsh expat who'd made Jamaica his home and produced a son, Gareth, who played a few times for the West Indies, and who now plies his trade for Durham CCC. Brian cared hugely for his adopted home.

Downtown Kingston was a tough area. The main government offices were still there, but there was huge dereliction as well, with both people and business having moved up to New Kingston and beyond to avoid the crime and poverty.

The meeting reminded me of one of those client meetings in advertising when they don't really want to see you, but with Courtney there, and with the backing and money of Britain's Department for International Development, they had got to see us.

One of the main problems facing the prison service in the UK, especially in prisons for young offenders, is the very high level of re-offending once the sentence is served – up to 80 per cent in some cases, which is obviously expensive and self-defeating. Evidence from pilot projects in the UK suggests that introducing sport in general to young offenders, and cricket in particular, can help improve their attitude and behaviour.

The meeting was interrupted by constant phone calls, documents being brought in to be signed, and 'news from the front'. I guess when you're running a prison service in an island short of money and dominated by crime there aren't many laughs to be had, so we faced a barrage of difficult questions (not just the obvious ones like: what happens when the ball goes over the fence? Answer: nothing). However, after a tough couple of hours it looked like a cautious yes to what we wanted – access to the island's jails to launch a cricket programme, not only to help the inmates but also to help the staff in looking after them.

The other programmes had been easier to organise because they built on Mikey's previous work in Jamaica. Only a few months later The Courtney Walsh Foundation was launched – a very grand affair, with the obligatory celebs guaranteeing the wall-to-wall publicity necessary to generate momentum quickly.

The event was held at the sports complex of the University of the West Indies at Mona, on the outskirts of Kingston. It was a world away from the deprivation of the inner-city. As is Jamaica's way, music played a key role, with all singing the Jamaican national anthem (much better than ours, but then most are) led by Abijah, a delightful young Rasta performer who then summed up the day's vibe by singing a song about peace that he'd written for the occasion.

A few participating prisoners had been allowed out for the day, leading to the old joke that they were something of a captive audience. Sorry. Thankfully, at the end of the festivities they were all counted back in, Brian Hanrahan-style, otherwise I'm sure we'd have been blamed.

The legendary fast bowler Wes Hall, now a reverend based in Florida, added some Bajan spice to the occasion with a rumbustious speech summing up all that's great about cricket. If only our sermons were like that. His inclusion in the event summed up the three powerful forces in Jamaica: religion, sport and music, which, when used appropriately, can help solve Jamaica's problems.

All this made us feel good about what we were embarking on, so much so that we enjoyed a few Red Stripes followed by some Appleton rum at the Confortania Lounge, to celebrate the day. Abijah performed more of his wistful songs about the future, and Mikey introduced us to his alter ego, 'Inspector Hotfoot', rapping for his supper by describing the events of the launch in the context of contemporary Jamaica.

His rapping language is more Jamaican patois than Peckham, and the reaction he got from the local crowd backed up his explanation for his striking stage name, which is that because a lot of his content is political (and politics is an extremely dangerous subject in Jamaica) he often has to hotfoot it away from venues to avoid being lynched.

A few days later we got a wonderful welcome at the Sir John Golding Disability Centre, not far from the Mona campus. The centre is part residential, part day care, and offers respite and rehabilitation for (mainly) adults with a whole range of physical disabilities. Despite its function, it's a happy place with a range of buildings set in a tree-shaded campus.

I love the trees in Jamaica. Most islands in the West Indies are pretty barren, with picture postcard palms and beaches, but Jamaica is high and hilly, so massive trees like the silk cotton provide shade, and the African Tulip's flame-coloured flowers burst out of the hillsides that surround Kingston. Jamaica's national flower comes from the *lignum vitae* – the tree of life – whose wood is so dense that it's used for the bails that replace light ones blown off by the wind

– another major contribution that Jamaica has given the game. Heavy, man.

Athletics is the main sport at the centre, supported by Jamaica's athletics excellence and the fact that it's a mainstay of the Paralympics. However, blind cricket has now become a major force in the Caribbean, with an annual inter-island competition mirroring that in the mainstream game, and it has support from the West Indies Cricket Board and the ICC.

But cricket for the physically disabled is more difficult to organise, because of the variety of disabilities and because there's no international recognition. If cricket, the Twenty20 version, were to become an Olympic sport, it would transform the opportunities available to the disabled in the sport, as Paralympics versions would inevitably follow. But the ICC is lukewarm, because every four years their precious schedules would be affected, a short-sighted view that will undoubtedly hold back the development of the game worldwide.

The introduction of cricket at the centre was big news, because they'd never had a chance to play before. Mikey has a knack of surreptitiously adapting the game to suit all sorts, so that no one feels embarrassed by what they can't do. In essence cricket is simple. Just hitting a ball with a stick, with all other aspects of the game subsidiary to that central fact, and as long as that can be achieved, fun can be had.

And fun was had. Most of the players were wheelchair-bound and were able to bowl and bat really well, while we help out with the fielding where needed. Two stars were Patrick and Susan. Patrick had been born with tiny arms and legs. He didn't come from a wealthy family so had never used a wheelchair, but shot around on a skateboard, putting our fielding to shame. He bowled with pinpoint accuracy, flicking the ball at some pace and often surprising the batsman, at which he unleashed the sort of evil grin that Muralitharan perfected. Murali's 'doosra' was one of his many baffling deliveries, but I reckon Patrick got there first. Susan was university educated and was a celebrated member of the Jamaica ladies cricket team before she lost the use of her legs in a serious car accident. She hadn't let her disability get in the way of her love and talent for the game, and she was the star of this cricketing show.

After an hour and a half's action, the Sun was starting to slip behind the Blue Mountains, so we packed up the kit, said cheerio till next week, and headed back to the comfort of the Confortania Lounge. Another good day.

While our work with disabled cricketers was simply about giving people a new opportunity to enjoy themselves, prison cricket has much broader aims and brings with it a very different set of challenges.

I'd never been inside a prison before I'd been to Jamaica. I'd driven past the red-brick walls of Leicester prison many times on my way to the Tigers, the County or the City, and we'd once shot a commercial for Bell's whisky at Wandsworth prison, but actually going through the gates, being searched, and having your camera, keys, money and phone taken off you was very unnerving, even though I knew I'd done nothing wrong.

The Rio Cobre Young Offenders Institution was named after the river that runs by it in a gorge on its way to the Caribbean. It didn't have the forbidding exterior that one might expect. Most of the young people were in lessons in the teaching blocks, next to which was a good-sized cricket ground surrounded by a high barbed-wire fence.

We were briefed about the boys and girls who were there. Some had committed crimes of one sort or another, but others were there simply because they were either 'out of control' or because there was nowhere else for them to go. In a way, the latter cases were the saddest as almost inevitably they were the product of broken homes.

I talked a lot to Carl, who shared the same surname as my wife's maiden name — a strange coincidence. He didn't seem a bad lad to me, but he'd been abandoned by his birth parents and then by his foster parents, so there was nowhere else for him. All he wanted was 'a nice home to live in', but he was already sixteen years old, and would be out in a year's time, with, presumably, nowhere to go.

He hoped the Jamaican army or police force would have him, as he was a strong young man, and they might be able to fulfil the role of a surrogate family that he needed. I hope one of them does, but I worry that they'd look at his record — 'Rio Cobre Young Offenders Institution' and then turn him down. I know what HR departments are like.

I thought of my own 'nice home' in Hertfordshire, which has got plenty of room for another 'son', and of the shared surnames. But I chickened out, maybe not wishing to be regarded as some kind of Madonna-like figure, or to be accused of favouritism, tokenism, or any number of other 'isms'.

Most of the kids had been shouted at for most of their lives, so their communication skills were limited, and most struggled with reading and writing because they had been excluded from schools because of their behaviour. The centre did a good job in giving the kids a structured life, thus helping their behaviour and in turn enabling teaching to have positive results. But the addition of cricket, using methods that had succeeded at Ashfield in Bristol, could also help with their behaviour and the development of social skills.

The game has various useful guiding principles: you should listen to the captain who's issuing the orders, obey the umpire who's making the decisions, and keep a tally of the score and the batsmens' and bowlers' figures. The latter are good mathematics training, with the whole game a metaphor for life. Winning some and losing some. Having good days as well as bad days. All these things are learned in the context of having fun, which is why people respond so positively.

These sound like grandiose claims for the game, but when we organised a match for the Rio Cobre Young Offenders Institution kids on their ground you could see that it worked. Fun and exercise were being had, and a good crowd of inmates and warders enjoyed the action. More importantly the structure of the game and its strange intricacies were also starting to impose a degree of order into the chaotic lives of young people whose experiences in the outside world had been mainly disorderly.

To try to stop some of these young kids getting into trouble, a series of inner-city programmes in Kingston have been started. These are based on successful similar schemes in London, funded by Barclays Bank, the Metropolitan Police

JAMAICA – 'ONE LOVE'

and the Cricket Foundation. Tapeball cricket is played, and informal guidance is given to the kids to steer them away from any potential trouble. It's much more difficult in Kingston, firstly because the same level of funding isn't in place, and secondly because the levels of deprivation are so much greater.

Bob Marley made Trench Town famous, but there are dozens of similar neighbourhoods in Kingston, such as Olympic Gardens and Tivoli Gardens, which sound nice, but which are forbidding places to walk through, let alone work in. As Mikey explained, 'Even the birds don't dare fly over these places.' One of our projects was in Nannyville, within sight of the Jamaica National Stadium, but also within earshot of gunfire, which often started as soon as the Sun goes down – the opposite of the dawn chorus. While the aims of the inner-city programme were properly set out in an 'official-ese' document, Mikey summed it up much more succinctly: 'We're here to hush de gun and hush de knife.'

The kids certainly seemed to listen to the good advice from the coaches, that about batting and bowling as well as 'hushing de gun'. Most attention was given to Ricardo, a young man who had done his spell at Rio Cobre (and so had serious ghetto cred) and who was now helping to spread the good word.

I innocently asked about a pair of trainers hanging from the overhead power lines, which seemed odd as some of the kids don't even possess a pair of their own. The answer surprised me: 'It's about respect.' They belonged to a young man who was murdered there a few weeks ago, and they were there as a shrine to his memory, just like the sad memorials at the side of the road in England that mark road deaths. This story encapsulated the scale of the problem we were dealing with. Violent death on the streets of Kingston is commonplace, almost casual, and is even regarded as a badge of honour.

The Jamaica *Sunday Observer* recently reported under the headline 'Kill or be Killed' that young men would do anything to avoid going to prison: 'If me and police clash, is either them or me, but me naaw go a prison. Dem haffi kill me fus.' In my work in advertising, changing human behaviour was the hardest thing to do, but in advertising it's just a case of one brand against another. In Kingston, it's life versus death, an altogether more important choice.

With this in mind, our first visit to Spanish Town jail took on added significance. Spanish Town, as its name suggests, was the capital of Jamaica when it was ruled by the Spanish. It declined over the years as the British capital, Kingston, with its huge natural harbour, grew at its expense. But it remained an important administrative centre, and the British built a formidable prison there in the nineteenth century, on mediaeval castle lines, which must have been quite a shock for the average Jamaican inmate.

Luckily, Courtney was with us on this first visit, which smoothed our way through the inevitable tough security. Walking around with Courtney in Jamaica must be rather like walking around with David Beckham in Los Angeles. He is instantly recognised and is well loved by all. Being 6' 7" helps too. Walking round Lord's with Courtney is an event as well. A couple of years back I was walking there with him on one side of me and Devon Malcolm on the other. Obviously they were both recognised the whole way round, and equally obviously I wasn't, but I did hear someone say to his chum 'Who's the old white guy in the middle of Courtney and Devon? It's not Harold Larwood, is it?'

Back in Spanish Town, despite the heat, the overcrowding and the reputation of the prisoners (it's a high-security prison), the atmosphere was surprisingly genial. One of the main problems of prisons, so they tell me, is the sheer boredom of it all, so a polyglot group of visiting dignitaries carrying a cricket bag was at least something new. It was mid-morning, and a reggae band was playing soulful music on one side of the huge central quadrangle, to which the warders were happily clapping along, even more so when Inspector Hotfoot decided to join in with his Spanish Town Jail Rap. Shades of Johnny Cash's famous Fulsome Jail concert, which brought the house down, if not the prison.

On the other side, lunch was being prepared in the cookhouse. It smelled good. Not that sophisticated, just two massive iron vats, one full of turkey neck curry, a cheap Jamaican staple affectionately known as 'ghetto steak', and the other full of rice. The Jamaicans don't seem to do vegetables, apart from rice and peas, so it can't be much fun being a veggie, as one of our party was, but at least I guess the repetitive diet separates the real veggies from the attention-seekers.

In anticipation of our visit, a hardball game of cricket was already underway in the quad, surprising really when both a cricket bat and a cricket ball could easily be classed as offensive weapons, particularly when being wielded by high-security prisoners. But this is Jamaica, where they still like their proper cricket, despite the attractions of other sports.

The players immediately asked Courtney, and us, to join in the game, which he was happy to do, as were we. I'd never played with him, and nor had most of the prisoners, although it happened that he knew the batsman well, as he'd played a few games for Jamaica, and was serving a long stretch for murdering his wife!

Courtney placed his field with great precision. Mikey asked to be close to the music, and I was put at mid-on. I know that you usually put your worst fielder at mid-on, who's just there as a go-between for the wicket-keeper and the bowler, but in this case it was important – I was guarding the cookhouse, which was apparently a popular target, since the inmates were always complaining about the food and about the 'trusties' who prepared it.

Courtney came in off a shortish run, although to be honest there wasn't really room for him to come off his long one, and the batsman didn't seem to be having much difficulty playing him, despite the dodgy pitch. You could see this batsman been a decent player, and, confidence growing, he lashed a ball towards the cookhouse. It was a bit uppish, and came at such a rate towards me that I couldn't avoid it. The ball just stuck in my right hand. 'Caught Rodwell bowled Walsh' was duly entered into my borrowed Bourne's Empire scorebook, which was recording the events for posterity. A proud moment, despite the fact that I'd ruined the batsman's day, and that if there'd been any way of avoiding the catch I certainly would have done.

Now we all know about the MCC's laudable Spirit of Cricket and all that, but as soon as I caught the ball, it crossed my mind what this particular batsman's reaction might be, bearing in mind that he was a convicted murderer wielding a wooden bat and that I was unarmed. He walked towards me. Would it be one of those Sue Barker *Question of Sport* 'What happened next?' moments? I suppose in a way it was, because what happened next was indeed somewhat unusual. He put his bat down, and shook my hand. 'Good catch, man.'

My immediate reaction was to apologise, true as ever to the MCC's Spirit of Cricket. Yet another excellent spell of bowling from Courtney — maybe not up to his 14-over spell at Sabina Park in 1994 against Atherton et al., which he reckons was his best, but certainly up there.

The luncheon interval, naturally, was turkey neck curry, which we enjoyed with the prisoners. One came up to me and asked how Croydon was these days, not the sort of question I was expecting. But he was one of the deported prisoners, and had been brought up in Croydon and remembered it fondly.

Not that many people remember Croydon fondly, but I guess it's normal that we hark back longingly to places where we were happy. Even though he was being treated well in Spanish Town jail, and was resigned to his fate, he knew that he'd never see Croydon again.

Tamarind Farm might sound like one of the Sandals Resorts that Jamaica is so famous for, but in fact it's a medium-security prison set in the countryside not far from Spanish Town.

In a sense, Tamarind Farm is what it says on the tin. Approached down a rural road next to a Grace Kennedy food processing plant, the entrance is shaded by a grove of tamarind trees. Like the cotton tree, the tamarind is omnipresent across the tropics and, according to Mikey, has a fruit that is a vital ingredient in both HP Sauce and Lea and Perrins Worcestershire Sauce. I had to check this out back home, as I love both products, and he was right, which increased my respect both for the Big Man, and, indeed, for the tamarind tree.

Past the tamarind trees is the farm, a field about as big as a football pitch growing tomatoes, potatoes, melons and peppers, all of which provide therapeutic work for the prisoners and make for a better diet too. Beyond the farm is the cricket pitch, bald red earth providing a lightning fast outfield and a bouncy wicket.

The inmates at Tamarind Farm are mainly drug dealers and carriers, so not the more dangerous big shots who fill the high-security prisons. Before the weekly match, we started with the prerequisite classroom lesson on respect and communication. They listened politely enough, but tended to come and go from the room with a range of more or less believable excuses. A few turned up late, true to the 'soon come' and 'Jamaica time' culture that is all-pervasive out there.

The warders didn't seem to mind – anything for an easy life I guess – and the only issue was with the sole white prisoner, a northerner who'd been caught bringing in cocaine. 'Ganja out, cocaine in' was the succinct description of the drug scene in Jamaica given to me by one of the warders. The white guy reckoned he'd been discriminated against by not being given good enough trainers to play in. I wasn't going to argue with him, so he stormed off in a huff.

It was his loss, as the game turned out to be a good one. I was umpiring, and the standard was high. A couple of the warders were playing too, not to keep order, but because they love playing. I was praying that my umpiring was up to scratch, to avoid any Gatting/Shakor Rana-type incidents, but thankfully there weren't any flashpoints, and the game approached a good climax, with the batting side needing only six to win off the last over, with three wickets remaining.

Kelly, a chubby, jovial character who had that wonderful ability to bowl straight, was bowling on a decent length. You miss and it hit. And miss they did, three batsmen facing Kelly's third, fourth and fifth deliveries, a hat trick, all bowled, which ended the game. High fives all round. I felt that Kelly deserved something by which to remember the day. All I could think of giving him were my sunglasses, a pretty ordinary gesture, but one which both he, and his team, loved. 'Thanks, man. Well umpired.' I'm sure that Kelly will go straight, hopefully as straight as his bowling, when his sentence is over.

We couldn't get to the women's and girls' prison, which also takes part in the cricket programme, so Tower Street prison in downtown Kingston was the final visit on this trip, and by far the most forbidding. Built from British red bricks brought in as ballast on the nineteenth century trading ships, it's by the harbour on the site of the original Kingston slave market that first made Jamaica rich. Some of the buildings from that slave market still survive in the Tower St complex, which is a terrible reminder to us of what we imposed on Jamaica, and to the inmates of the area's troubled past.

Mikey reckons that the reason Jamaica has produced so many tremendous sportsmen is that those who survived the Middle Passage across the Atlantic must have been the strongest, and that the Kingstonian slave owners took the pick of those survivors before the remainder of the cargo were taken to the other islands. I've no idea whether that's true, but sadly, it makes sense.

Like Spanish Town, Tower St is high-security, being the home to many convicted murderers, including those who killed Pete Tosh, one of Bob Marley's Wailers, and Trevor Berbick, who for a while was world heavyweight boxing champion.

Although the Tower St cricket ground was small, surrounded by a high barbed-wire fence, the cricket team was as keen as mustard, although still smarting from a narrow nine-run defeat at the hands of the visiting Tamarind Farm team the previous week. The Tower St team was not allowed to travel to away fixtures – I'd love that, as there's nothing worse than driving for miles only to get beaten – so the Tamarind Farm team had been brought in by a convoy of buses (security said that each should carry only four prisoners, accompanied by two warders). The buses had been escorted by motorcycle outriders on the twenty-mile journey, paralysing the traffic along the way. If that had happened in England there would have been an uproar, but in Jamaica crowds cheered them along the route, Tour de France style.

After we'd finished the session, one of the prisoners, Rohan, gave me an envelope to take way. 'Open it later,' he said. I did, somewhat apprehensively. It was a letter, countersigned by the prison governor, thanking us for all our work, and wishing us a safe journey home. This not only gave me a good feeling inside, but it also bodes well for the future, for despite the tough circumstances of everyone in Tower St prison, amazingly some good manners had survived.

Of course, the 'other side' of Jamaica does exist. We joined Courtney's Melbourne Cricket Club's annual harbour cruise, which was a wonderfully vibrant few hours spent drinking rum and jigging about under the stars. The following morning we were due to play a game against Mikey's village, Water Lane in Clarendon, and we were still two players short. So a couple of fellow revellers on the boat agreed to play, Jimmy Adams and Ian 'Tippy' Hinds, brother of Wavell, who'd also played for Jamaica.

Despite the previous evening's rum, we all met up at 8am the following morning ('Jamaica time' doesn't exist as far as cricket is concerned) for the long journey west. I found myself batting with Jimmy on a ground where there were as many chickens and goats as players. After every ball I faced, Jimmy gave me a batting masterclass, but after half an hour his patience ran out, so he ran me out, as I just couldn't hit it off the square. He bade me a cheery 'Sorry, Tom' as I trudged off. Still, the fact that an ex-West Indies captain is happy to spend his Sunday playing with country boys and English village cricketers just for the *craic* sums up all that's good about the Jamaican character.

That week also coincided with the Jamaica Boys and Girls Athletic Championships at the National Stadium, an incredibly well organised event where the cream of Jamaica's young athletic talent from over 100 participating schools strut their stuff in front of an audience of fanatical family and friends, as well as talent-spotting US college coaches. Usain Bolt's 20.25sec 200m record set in 2003 still stands, so there was everything to run for, especially as he was there to cheer everyone on – another example of the generous Jamaican spirit.

The memories of this event, the village cricket match, the prison cricket and the disabled cricket were all whirring around my mind when we wrapped up at Courtney's sports bar and restaurant, Cuddyz, in New Kingston. Despite the country's problems, sport is still alive and well in Jamaica, and the nation still has the ability to create great events, great stars and great sporting venues. The new Sabina Park, where we saw the Jamaica team give the England Lions a good game, is a wonderful place to watch cricket. Both we and Courtney are convinced that the work that his foundation is doing will, over time, help Jamaica develop as a nation, with sport and music leading the way.

The response we'd had in Jamaica to our disability cricket, cricket in the ghettos, and in prisons made me feel that our efforts were helping. We began to wonder if we could take this pragmatic approach to other countries to see how cricket could help there as well – perhaps even in places where the sport wasn't as well established as it was in Jamaica.

Our British government friends in Jamaica seemed to be of the same opinion and mentioned that there might be an opportunity to do some work in Cuba, a place not far from Jamaica geographically, but a world away in terms of its history and its relationship with cricket.

4

CUBA – THIRD MAN
IN HAVANA

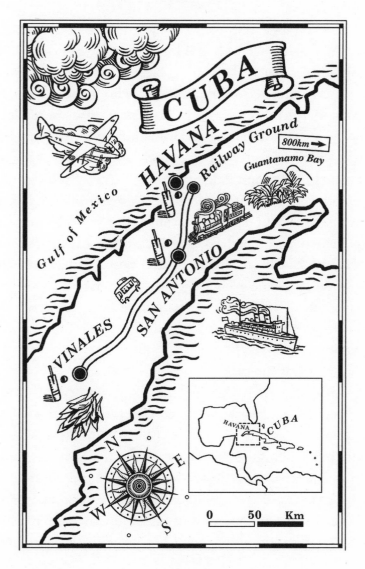

CUBA MIGHT APPEAR to be the most unlikely of the Caribbean islands on which to develop cricket, but we went there at the behest of the British government in a scheme which Mr Wormold, the blundering vacuum cleaner salesman-cum-spy in Graham Greene's *Our Man in Havana*, would have been proud of.

Greene didn't like sport much; indeed, his biographer Norman Sherry says, 'He didn't play games well, he found games particularly unpleasant.' This was confirmed by his daughter, Caroline Bourget, who I met at his old school Berkhamsted, where his father was headmaster. However, she said that he had some fun with his distaste for cricket in *Stamboul Train* in which two dodgy characters are called Hobbs and Zudgliffe (*sic*), after England's greatest opening partnership. Greene is well known in Cuba. Indeed, one of their most famous novelists, Pedro Juan Gutierrez, has written a somewhat scurrilous book called *Our GG in Havana*. But even Greene would probably have rejected the Foreign Office plan to reintroduce cricket to Cuba – in order to reduce American influence in the baseball-mad island – as being far too outlandish a plotline for a work of fiction.

But that was the plan.

Surprisingly, there has been a long history of British involvement in Cuba, and, indeed, of cricket in Cuba. Britain occupied the island for ten months in 1762; and Winston Churchill, when visiting Cuba to cover the Spanish/Cuban War as a journalist in 1895, said: 'It may be that future years will see the island as it would be now, had England never lost it – a Cuba free and prosperous under just laws and patriotic administration, throwing open her ports to the commerce of the world, sending her ponies to Hurlingham and her cricketers to Lord's.'

Churchill was surprisingly prescient, because in the 1920s and 1930s this is what almost happened, as thousands of West Indians, many keen on cricket, flocked to Cuba looking for work. Michael Manley states in his magisterial *History of West Indies Cricket*, 'During the 1920s more than 200,000 Jamaicans, Haitians and others went to Cuba to harvest the sugar crop which was growing larger every year.'

Also, 'British' West Indian labour was brought in by the Americans to build the now infamous Guantanamo naval base on the east of the island, and another tranche of West Indians arrived in Cuba from Panama, having finished building the canal. In this latter group was a young George Headley, who certainly played baseball in Cuba, although there's no record of his playing cricket there.

Most of these West Indian immigrants, having brought their love of cricket with them, set up clubs in the 'working' towns of Banes, Santiago, Manati, Baragua and Guantanamo, while Havana's 'high society' adopted the game as an amusing new way to while away the hours, much like Edwardian country house cricket in England.

Added credibility was given to the burgeoning game by the arrival of English multi-millionaire Sir Julien Cahn's famous touring cricket team, who squeezed Cuba into their Jamaican itinerary in 1928. Sir Julien was persuaded by the British ambassador to present a trophy, the Sir Julien Cahn Cricket Challenge Cup, to the winner of the grand final of the various leagues now centred on Havana, Guantanamo and Santiago. This was played for right up to the 1950s, by which time cricket teams from the Bahamas and Jamaica were also touring the island.

But decline set in, partly following Castro's revolution in 1959, which led to Jamaica breaking diplomatic relations, and partly through the falling interest in cricket among second generation Cuban West Indians – 'jamaiquinos' – who adopted more 'Cuban American' sports such as baseball and basketball. A similar thing is happening now in both England and the West Indies, with the interest of young black men in cricket declining. By the 1970s, only one game was being played annually, on 1 August each year at Baragua, to mark Emancipation Day for the mainly black players. By 1975 even that fixture had ended.

That the game was even capable of resuscitation was due to the efforts of one woman of Jamaican/Bajan extraction, Leona Ford, whose father Leonard had founded Guantanamo Cricket Club back in the 1920s.

In the 1990s a new influx of young West Indians was arriving in Cuba to study at their excellent universities, and Jamaica was keen to re-establish contact as Cuba struggled in the post-Soviet era. Indeed, Courtney Walsh visited the island several times to advise the Cubans and in 2000 the then British ambassador organised a game between the embassy staff and the locals. By 2002 Leona Ford had persuaded the ICC to award Cuba affiliate status.

Leona is most impressive, a woman who supported the revolution by working for many years in Ethiopia, and whose university specialisation in English had enabled her to travel widely – back to Jamaica, as well as to the US, Canada and the UK.

Many of the now third-generation blacks in Cuba are at the bottom of their so-called egalitarian society ('jamaiquino' is a somewhat derogatory term in Spanish); indeed, there's a West Indian Welfare Association to look after their interests. Fidel and Raul Castro came from a white middle-class background as did most of the early leaders – Che Guevara was an Argentinian doctor – but Leona's fierce intellect, striking looks and combative personality forced the authorities to take notice of her, when she invoked Fidel Castro's early policy statement that 'Sport is the Right of the People'. So much so that by 2006 cricket was adopted as Cuba's 38th official sport, which allowed it to be taught in schools.

But why on earth would the British government be interested in supporting the reintroduction of cricket to Cuba? Well, this is where we return to 'Greeneland', a murky world invented by Graham Greene, where intrigue and subterfuge rule.

US policy towards Cuba since Kennedy's 1961 Bay of Pigs fiasco has been to try to isolate it from the rest of the capitalist world, and the rest of the world hasn't dared to intervene, even though Cuba is no longer a threat to US security, if it ever was. The Castro regime still holds sway, though now it's in the hands of Fidel's brother Raul. Received wisdom sees the US circling the island like a vulture, ready to pile back in at the first sign of the regime faltering.

But our valiant Foreign Office had another idea. Why not get the Cubans playing cricket again? Link them up with our West Indian former colonies, so that post-Castro they'll be our friends and not patsies of the US. Now I hasten to add, in order to avoid prosecution under the Official Secrets Act, that this is my surmise of the situation, and that if there's any official documentation to support this policy, then without doubt it will be held under lock and key for at least 50 years, and not even a Freedom of Information request will succeed in ascertaining the real truth.

The devilish scheme involves an exchange of sports coaches in boxing, judo and cricket put together by top levels of government at both ends. Heading up the Cuban side was their vice-minister of sports, Alberto Juantorena, who when winning, uniquely, both the 400m and 800m gold medals at the 1976 Olympics was famously described by David Coleman as 'opening his legs and showing his class'. Alberto certainly showed his class by allowing cricket into this cosy arrangement, probably without realising the plot behind it.

Apparently the Cubans are ace at judo, and have certainly produced a string of brilliant boxers, such as Teofilio Stevenson and more recently Mario Kindelan, who beat Amir Khan to the gold at the 2004 Olympics. But the bold inclusion of cricket in the Foreign Office's cunning plan was welcomed by all the Cubans involved, in a country which is crazy about sport, but which has been starved of international competition since being abandoned by both the US and the former Soviet states.

The Soviet legacy remains, however, and our pioneering cricketing jaunt had to be part of a rigorous five-year plan for the game. This had been prepared by the Cuban sports ministry, INDER, who had no knowledge whatsoever of the game or its intricacies.

Now I know that sports governing bodies in the UK are routinely chastised for knowing little about the sports that they govern, but the Cuban five-year plan for cricket had been put together with great fastidiousness by Wilma, a short fat woman of mixed race from INDER who didn't seem at all happy in her job. She was constantly bickering with Leona, who did know what she was talking about, but had to kowtow to the strictures of the government department – a familiar scenario in England, but taken to extremes in Cuba.

The plan was certainly comprehensive, involving umpiring and scoring seminars at the sports university in Havana, coach education, schools cricket, adult cricket, international cricket, and cricket for the disabled. We were also asked to help set up an entire cricket infrastructure, from a cricket bat manufacturing facility to advice in isolating sites for cricket pitches and their development and maintenance.

We were wildly unsuited to perform the latter tasks, having none of the specialist knowledge required, but, egged on by the Foreign Office, we threw ourselves into all our allotted roles with gusto.

As the oldest of our merry group, and having done a bit of university lecturing, I was given the task of explaining the laws of the game and the intricacies of scoring to the assembled group of putative administrators, umpires and scorers at the Havana Sports University, a facility built by the Soviets on a grand scale in the 1960s, but which, like a lot of things in Cuba, had seen better days.

It's always nerve-racking speaking to a group of strangers in a formal situation, but doubly so when they don't understand a word you're saying, and when you aren't too familiar with your subject. I'd been prescient enough to undertake a short course in umpiring and scoring at Dulwich Cricket Club, and had bought a pristine copy of *Tom Smith's New Cricket Umpiring and Scoring*. I thought Tom Smith made Christmas crackers, but obviously he'd branched out into cricket.

The MCC had also kindly provided some copies of the Laws of Cricket in Spanish, but the three-hour sessions in the classroom soon descended into chaos as Wilma and Leona argued about the interpretation of the laws and the correct terms in Spanish, while I valiantly attempted to explain the LBW law and the signal for a short run.

The strangeness of cricket as a game is brought into sharp relief when one starts to discuss fielding positions with people who have no knowledge of the game and who don't speak English. It was when I illustrated the position 'third man' on my flip chart that I realised the madness of what we were attempting. A look of puzzlement came over my group as 'third man' was translated to them.

A hand went up with a question. 'If there's a third man, then where is the first man and the second man?' I gave a rambling answer, saying that I thought that originally 'third man' referred to what we'd now call second slip, with the wicketkeeper being the 'first man', and first slip 'second man', but that third man is generally now back towards the boundary on the offside, often, in the sort of cricket that I play, with his hands in his pockets. A pretty unsatisfactory answer that even my English colleagues didn't fully understand.

All I could think about was books. Firstly, there were the inadequacies of Tom Smith's book, which had failed me in these admittedly trying circumstances, and secondly Graham

Greene's two books, *The Third Man* and *Our Man in Havana*, which in my deluded state I somehow felt mirrored my own situation.

I'd read *Our Man in Havana* — Greene's book about a failed English spy in the city just before Castro's revolution — on the plane over. I had also recently seen the movie version starring Alec Guinness again. Both had whet my appetite for Cuba. *The Third Man* — Greene's story which was made into an atmospheric film set in post-Second World War Vienna where crime and deception were rampant — had also re-entered my psyche for its unintentional cricketing connection.

I found myself in a trance. I began to wonder whether I was being used by the Foreign Office as a 21st century version of the hapless Mr Wormold in *Our Man in Havana* — part of a game even bigger than cricket; the very political future of Cuba and its place in the Caribbean world. Was I, in fact, the 'Third Man in Havana', one of those outsiders so common in Greene, with a mission to fulfil?

My reverie was interrupted and I was brought crashing back to earth as Wilma and Leona promptly started arguing over the respective field placings of third man and long-leg, with the bemused students listening and watching attentively.

Despite the language problems (and my delusions of grandeur) the students seemed to be enjoying themselves, as it was a treat for them to be taken out of their various day jobs as teachers, sports coaches, secretaries and such like. They were young and old, men and women, black, white and mixed race, a true reflection of Cuba's polyglot society where everyone seems to rock on pretty amicably together, despite racial differences and over 50 years of tough times as an outcast on the world stage.

Over the next few weeks, some of the participating students – Emiliano, Coralia, Danielys, Felix, Ivan, Reinaldo and Yohanadris – became firm friends of mine, and while I certainly enjoyed all they taught me about life in Cuba, I think they in turn enjoyed being introduced to a new sport and to new friends from England.

Although Cuba and Jamaica are only 100 miles or so from each other, the contrast between the two countries is enormous. Obviously, Spanish colonial influence rather than British is one reason for this, but equally the histories of the two over the past 50 years could not be more different. Castro's regime in Cuba is still hardline communist, with rigid planning and discipline, and a huge respect for education and healthcare, whereas Jamaica's fractious two-party system since independence has taken the island to the brink of chaos. The net result is that both islands are poor, but at least Cuba feels safe, a welcome positive side effect to an otherwise extremely disciplinarian regime.

A feast of cricket had been planned to coincide with our visit, including a resurrection of the old needle match between Havana and Guantanamo. This was to be the first trial as to whether my umpiring and scoring masterclass had had any positive effect, let alone whether the participants could actually play the game.

Havana was always the posh team in the old days, whereas Guantanamo was the working-class side from the other end of the island, a sort of latter-day Middlesex v Yorkshire. The Guantanamo team had travelled the 500 or so miles along the length of the island overnight. We tend to think of Caribbean islands as tiny, but Cuba is about the same size as the UK, so their fifteen-hour journey in a rickety yellow American school bus from the 1950s was testament to their keenness.

The match was taking place at the Havana Sports University, on a baseball diamond across which had been laid a Flicx brand artificial pitch that had just arrived, from South Africa at our behest, courtesy of the Foreign Office.

The restrictions on imports into Cuba are bewildering, partly because of the US and partly because of notorious Cuban red tape. Perhaps understandably the West has been worried about what enters Cuba since Krushchev sent missiles by ship in 1961, prompting the Cuban missile crisis. Now, while an artificial cricket pitch would not normally be regarded as a threat to Western, or indeed Cuban society, you never know, so the pitch had been despatched in the diplomatic bag in order to avoid any possible Cuban cricket pitch crisis. Apparently this was the first time in history that a cricket pitch had been sent via the diplomatic bag, a Foreign Office first of which we were naturally proud to be part.

Our Foreign Office friends said that the diplomatic bag is routinely used to send British necessities across the world, but that normally it contains essentials such as Colman's mustard, Marmite and Tizer, which admittedly are much more dangerous items than cricket pitches. We suggested that in future the diplomatic bag should be called the 'cricket bag', at which the Foreign Office types smiled wanly.

The game took a while to organise as quite a crowd had gathered to see what on earth we were up to. Emiliano was chosen as the home umpire as he seemed to look the part – a cross between Ernest Hemingway and Ernesto 'Che' Guevara. This proved to be a big mistake, as every decision he made was subject to negotiation. This particularly annoyed Guantanamo's opening bowler who rejoiced in the surname of Stalin, and was as bad-tempered and aggressive as his Soviet namesake. The Guantanamo team had tried to include a few ringers from the eponymous prison, which is apparently full of fine Pakistani and Afghan cricketers, but the killjoy Americans had refused.

LBW has never been my strong suit, but I had to intervene on one decision which was plainly out. The batsman concerned, one Signor Lopez, had refused to leave the wicket and embarked on a dramatic strop that was matched only by Stalin's furious temper. I feared an international incident of 'bodyline' proportions was about to erupt, and it was only the intervention of the watching Cuban Director of Recreation, José, that saved the day as he reminded all of the Spirit of the Revolution, on which I now realise the MCC's Spirit of Cricket is loosely based.

He repeated Fidel's words declaimed at the beginning of 1959: 'The Revolution must concentrate on sport. Youngsters of outstanding talent will be plucked from the masses and will be given the best training [an obvious reference to my scoring and umpiring masterclasses, which I acknowledged with a self-satisfied smile]. On the front line of sport the Revolution will advance. Fatherland or death. We will win.'

So he was out then.

I vowed to repeat these fine words next time my team were misbehaving in England, but they somehow lose resonance if you're not wearing military uniform, surrounded by heavily armed bodyguards and sporting a beard W.G. Grace would have been proud of.

The scoring was going much better, partly because the Cuban education system is strong on maths, and partly because the keenest scorer was a very pretty 20-year-old Cuban girl called Danielys, who was wearing a tight t-shirt and unfeasibly tiny shorts. As most seasoned cricketers will concur, a pretty cricket scorer is a relatively rare phenomenon, although in the unlikely event that my wife reads this, she was, with Danielys, one of the two exceptions that prove the rule.

We hung on Danielys' every word. '*Una carrera a* third man?' she trilled, proving that she'd hung on my every word too, as she accurately inserted all the correct details into my Bourne's 'Empire' scorebook.

It was a low-scoring game, mainly because the batting was pretty dreadful. Cubans are great baseball players, but the cross-batted swing is rarely an effective substitute for a classic front-foot drive when, unlike in baseball, the ball normally bounces before it gets to you. But the bowling was surprisingly good, with not too much throwing, although everything was hurled down at a furious pace, especially by the increasingly irascible Stalin. I still couldn't get used to Stalin's name, but in retrospect it only follows the great West Indian tradition of naming sportsmen after political leaders, hence Gladstone Small, Franklin Stephenson and Dwight Yorke.

Havana had amassed a total of only 56, with Stalin taking five-for, but Guantanamo's innings also stuttered, and in one of those coincidences that seem usually to happen only in books, they tied on 56, which at least saved the watching José from having to intervene again.

Danielys was embraced by everyone – well, all the men anyway – and she surprisingly beat Stalin to win the '"man" of the match' award, having scored so beautifully. Who scored with Danielys later that evening must, however, remain a Secret of the Revolution, as this, after all, is a cricket book.

The Havana team soon disappeared back to their homes on foot and by bus, bike and moped, so the Guantanamo boys were left kicking their heels. None of them had any money, and they were being put up at the university, so we decided that that night should be Guantanamo Cricket Club's Annual Dinner in Havana, and that we should pay for it.

Leona suggested that a derelict club by the beach would make a good venue and that she could source music from the West Indian Welfare Association. Wilma was put off the scent by being sent to an alternative venue the other side of Havana. We had a whip-round and bought a pile of pizzas, fruit, Havana Club rum, Cuban cola, Cristal beer for the regular drinkers and strong Bucanero beers for Stalin and his ilk.

The presentation ceremony assuaged Stalin's disappointment at not being made man of the match as he was given a special award for his five-for, thus restoring one's faith in natural justice. At this, he smiled almost imperceptibly, a first since we'd met him – truly a victory for the Cricket Revolution.

One of the problems of cricket dinners back home is the interminable speeches, and this dinner was no exception, but at least the Cubans have a good excuse, having been brought up on Fidel Castro's day-long perorations.

Although the evening had been a good one, the length of the speeches meant that we didn't get to Mikey's *pièce de résistance* until dawn was breaking over Havana Bay. I wondered what he'd been doing all day, as most of it had been spent sitting under an acacia tree, but of course his alter ego Inspector Hotfoot had been working on his 'Guantanamo Rap', a fiercely anti-American diatribe that even those with minimal English could easily understand, and which was received with tumultuous applause as we united against 'the common enemy'.

So, after an eventful first day's cricket it seemed, even to this doubting Thomas, that the Foreign Office's devilish plan might just work.

The following day it was back to the five-year plan with a visit to the putative cricket bat factory in Vinales, and the site for an out-of-town ground at San Antonio de los Baños.

Driving through rural Cuba is wonderful. Not only is the lush countryside a great antidote to Havana's urban scrum, but there's hardly any traffic — the famous 1950s American cars being restricted mainly to taxi work in the tourist areas. So, bullocks pull carts through the tobacco plantations that supply Cuba's famous cigar-makers, and in the higher areas coffee to rival Jamaica's finest grows in individually tended plots.

Claudio the bat-maker in Vinales had a workshop at the top of a building which bizarrely could only be reached by a rickety ladder that had to be pulled up behind us, drawbridge-style. It was a particular struggle for Wilma – the seams on her Lycra jump suit were stretched to breaking point – but a team effort, which she seemed to rather enjoy, got her up there eventually, rather like getting a reluctant racehorse into the starting stalls. We were warming to Wilma, who although riotously unsuited to the job in hand nevertheless was starting to see the funny side of what we were being asked to do.

It turned out that Claudio was one of Cuba's leading baseball bat manufacturers and that the elaborately protected entrance to his workshop was to warn off potential industrial saboteurs. Cuban bats are highly prized even in the American NBA and obviously his trade secrets were worth protecting, even though we wouldn't know what to do with them.

There followed a long discussion, with no interpreter, about the relative properties of the baseball bat and the cricket bat. Claudio had never seen a cricket bat before and he was astounded at its construction, which was very different from a baseball bat. We'd brought with us a 'deconstructed' cricket bat, which he plainly thought was a ridiculous piece of equipment.

Baseball bats are made from one piece of wood, often ash or hickory, whereas the best cricket bats are made from English willow with a cane handle and a rubber grip. We had to try to persuade Claudio that the two-piece construction was essential to prevent jarring, and that it shouldn't be too difficult to source cane as half the island was covered in sugar cane. He wasn't convinced and seemed to indicate that there was nothing in the MCC laws of the game to demand two-piece construction. Where on earth he'd got this information from I don't know, but when I checked later I found that he's actually correct.

Willow doesn't grow in Cuba, but Claudio reckoned that the ceiba tree would work just as well, as its wood is soft and light, like willow. But as the ceiba tree grows to well over a 100ft, and in olden days used to be worshipped as a god, it struck us as a possibly inappropriate use for such a fine tree. After some hours we felt that the discussion had gone on long enough, so we left our deconstructed bat with him. As he pulled up the ladder behind us, we saw him gently shaking his head.

Our next stop was San Antonio de los Baños, an attractive town full of fountains and wells. This is where we met Rocky, the sports coach at the local school who had been telling his charges about cricket in advance of our arrival. Rocky, as his name suggests, was a keen boxer and even keener on his body, which rippled convincingly beneath his 'I'm a sports coach' kit. But the schoolchildren obviously loved him. They were surprisingly well prepared for our coaching session and practice match before 'the big one' in Havana the following day against the townie kids.

While the school buildings and facilities in San Antonio were ramshackle, the children themselves were fantastically smart, with immaculate uniforms and smiley faces. Their cricket was smart too. All they needed was a series of demonstrations of the basics, and such was their innate sporting talent that it was then hard to pick a team to represent the town the following day. The smiles of those selected were followed by a few tears from those who weren't. Sport is tough, at every level.

Before returning to Havana, Rocky took us to the site of the proposed new 'country' ground, a flat stretch of farmland by the main road. There was a stone-built cowshed shaded by palm trees there, which seemed a ready-made pavilion. We were excited by the prospect of bringing teams out here to play, and there had been talk of the British government paying for the ground's development. Mikey had been delegated as our group's 'pitch consultant', as he'd once been on a groundsman's course. He gave the site the thumbs up, so it was everyone back on the bus to Havana.

A posse of bigwigs was expected at the Centro Deportivo Ferroviario the following day for the regional schools match, but following a flurry of phone calls from London, that posse was somewhat bigger than forecast.

The Ferroviario ground was a 1930s Art Deco sports and social centre built for the railway company when times were obviously good. However, like everything else in Cuba it was slowly crumbling. The commuter trains still rattled by the boundary fence past dozens of derelict railway carriages, and the baseball diamond had obviously been recently used, but the two-storey pavilion into which the two teams and their retinues filed was virtually derelict.

We'd expected our friend José, the Director of Recreation, and the British ambassador to turn up. But about an hour before play I got a call from an old pal, Harry, who worked for Ken Livingstone, then Mayor of London. He asked if I was in Havana and had I heard that Ken was also in town for an IOC meeting before going to Venezuela to sign his much-heralded 'oil for buses' deal with President Chavez. I said yes to both questions, so Harry continued with his proposal.

I know this is going to sound ridiculous, but as we all know truth is stranger than fiction, so I shall continue with some background to the story. The oil deal had been in the offing for months and was seen as demonstrating that Ken's socialist principles could nevertheless lead to a good deal for London — cheap oil for its buses. In order to witness the groundbreaking deal, the world's media — BBC, Sky, Reuters, CNN, etc. — had been assembled in Cuba before being ferried across to Venezuela. Unfortunately, the deal had been called off at the last minute, as it coincided with a tricky pre-election period for Chavez, so Ken, his apparatchiks and, crucially, the world's media were at a loose end without a story to report.

I'd had some dealings with Ken years before at my advertising agency, where we'd done some ads to support the old GLC, and his people had been helpful in supporting the charity in London. Still, the favour being asked of me seemed to come straight out of a Graham Greene novel. Harry asked if Ken and his entourage could turn up at the ground to demonstrate his solidarity with the Cuban people and his love of sport, in this case cricket. This would make a nice headline for the world's press, and soften the blow of the cancellation of the Venezuelan deal.

Harry promised me a lunch on my return to London, which was enough for me to agree. A moment later my phone rang again. This time it was Simon, Ken's *chargé d'affaires*, asking for directions to the ground, just like members of my village cricket team used to do. A chap from the British embassy helped me out on this, and half an hour later a stream of large black Mercedes purred into the ground.

Harry suggested that when Ken arrived I should greet him as a long-lost friend, as that's what he would be doing to me. It seemed churlish not to – in for a penny, in for a pound – so as Ken got out of his car we hugged. The cameras whirred and snapped as he said some suitable words about the power of sport to do good, particularly among young people. Ken is not a renowned sports lover, but he had seen the power of sport to lift the nation when he was part of the London Olympic bid team, so there was some honesty in what he said.

We then walked around the ground – anti-clockwise as proper cricket people do – and chatted about the old days and Harry's astonishing request which had brought us together again. It made us both chuckle. Politics aside, Ken is an interesting man and it didn't bother me that we were being used for his purposes, as it made for a good story for us with the UK media. He stayed to watch a number of overs of enthusiastic play by the schoolchildren before he, his entourage and the world's media departed for hastily rearranged flights back to London.

Back in the pavilion of the Ferroviario ground to get out of the sun, I came across a discarded copy of Lenin's *La Alianza de la Clase Obrera y del Campesinado* (The Alliance of the Working Class with the Peasantry) – but unfortunately Ken had gone before I could share it with him.

That evening we relaxed at La Casa de la Musica with more Cristal beers and Havana Club before yet another big day – the quadrangular international tournament between England, Cuba, India and the West Indies, back at the Sports University. The Indian team was made up of their embassy staff and was surprisingly weak, although several were wearing work clothes to play in which was a bit of a giveaway. The West Indian team was strong, made up of mainly university medical students from across the West Indies. Cuba has a tremendous reputation for medical education (after all, Che Guevara was an Argentinian doctor) and provides doctors across the Caribbean and Central America.

But the big game was Cuba against an England XI, playing for the Sir Julien Cahn Trophy. Amazingly, the previous year, during an Easter spring clean, the original trophy from 1929 had been discovered in a dusty cupboard in the British embassy. It was now displayed on the boundary, being played for for the first time in over 40 years. This was a nice turn of fate, for it was Sir Julien's grandson who had first introduced me to the world of 'cricket with a purpose' all those years ago in India.

I was in the England XI, my first international selection, some 50 years after I first played the game. Obviously a late developer. Mikey was skippering, a somewhat controversial decision as although born in Enfield, North London, he'd spent more of his life in Jamaica than England. But he's a commanding figure wherever he goes, so I was happy with him in charge. We waited for our field placings.

Mikey always calls me Major, as a homage to David Bowie's 'Ground control to Major Tom', although to be honest I was never much of a Bowie fan. 'Third man, Major Tom,' he said. That was it; at last I *was* 'Third Man in Havana' and my day was made. After that, to be honest, I was so pleased to be third man, hands in pockets, that the game somewhat passed me by.

A total of 109 was never going to be enough for Cuba, let down by their baseball-style batting again, and they couldn't cope with the military medium bowling of our imbedded *Telegraph* journalist Tony Francis, another son of Leicester, who took a remarkable five for nineteen, which made his day too. The returning Stalin was suitably aggressive at the start of our innings, but after a couple of scares we managed a good win with only five wickets down and proudly held aloft Sir Julien's trophy.

That evening we were all entertained by the hospitable Indians at their embassy, where their larger-than-life ambassador was resplendent in a lime green sari, showing no signs of the curry stains the rest of us suffered as we scoffed our first good meal for a while. The evening finished with the showing of a Bollywood movie, which we had to endure while really all wanting to get back to the Casa de la Musica. By then we'd decided to call ourselves the Buena Vista Cricket Club in honour of our hosts and we were planning our own cricket dinner there with some good music.

The final day on tour is always a sad one, a bit like the last day of your summer holiday. I know we were meant to have been working, but it hadn't really felt like it. The Cubans seemed pleased with our work and even Wilma was smiling and exchanging pleasantries with Leona and José.

All those who had participated in our various coaching sessions and matches, young and old, had been invited to a special presentation at the Acapulco cinema, a florid 1950s building in the centre of town. We all had to sit through another movie, although this time a good British cricket one called *Wondrous Oblivion* about Jamaican and Jewish immigrants in London (with Spanish subtitles).

The children seemed to love it, as it made sense of the strange game to which they'd been introduced, and then, after the film, one by one, we were invited on to the stage to receive our 'Reconocimiento' – certificate of gratitude – from the Grupo de Desarollo de Cricket en Cuba (The Association for the Development of Cricket in Cuba). It is now hanging proudly on my office wall.

There are several postscripts to the Cuban story.

A week or two after our return, I received an email from Ivan Otley, one of the Guantanamo contingent who'd still got a bit of English, remembered from his grandfather. He wrote: 'In name of all the Guantanamos that participated in the recently seminary want to express you our gratitude and happiness for your friendship with us. We felt very nice with all the instructions that you gave us; we assure you that all will be apply with love in our game and transmission to the rest of our players.'

He also asked for a set of dominoes. The game is played everywhere across the Caribbean, but apparently the five-year plan for domino production had hit the buffers and there was a shortage across the entire island. He asked if I could send them to the British embassy for them to pass on, as he didn't trust the Cuban customs. Naturally I was happy to do this, and thereby increase even further the reputation of our wonderful embassy in Havana. With everything that's been happening at Guantanamo over recent years, it was good to bring a bit of sunshine to the lives of good Guantanamos like Ivan.

Later that year, as agreed in the five-year plan, a Cuban coach came across to England for a month to learn more about the game. His name was Michel, and we thought it was strange that we hadn't met him on our trip – we were expecting Rocky to be the chosen one.

Michel stayed with me for a while, as he had no money, and I took him down to my club, Berkhamsted, to play in a fourth team game. He was absolutely hopeless and had no knowledge of the game whatsoever, and no English either, both of which came as a surprise. It turned out that his specialisms at Havana Sports University were rock climbing, fishing, camping and orienteering, none of which has any connection whatsoever with a ball game where hand–eye coordination is a prerequisite. But this scenario exemplifies the madness of the system under the revolution. Michel was 'next cab on the rank' for a foreign sporting trip, irrespective of the experience needed, and the system is so rigid that it cannot be broken, however daft the outcome is. He was Wilma's revenge.

The third postscript is probably the saddest. After our

efforts and the decent performance of the Cuban cricketers, Cuba, with the Turks and Caicos Islands, was invited to take part in the inaugural Stanford Twenty20 tournament in the West Indies, which is exactly the sort of outcome that the Foreign Office's devilish plan was intended to achieve.

Although Stanford has since been discredited and jailed, this would have been a fantastic first experience for the Cubans – to take part in international West Indies cricket, with the promise of money to help develop the game and Jamaican coaches to take over where we left off. But because Stanford was a US citizen, the US boycott of all things Cuban meant that they were banned from entering a team. Now, with the demise of Stanford, and the West Indies themselves in some disarray, Cuba remains on the outside looking in. But there is undoubtedly fantastic sporting talent on the island, which, if developed, would add to the lustre of West Indian cricket.

The final postscript is perhaps the most interesting, for it led directly to our next (even more unlikely), escapade in the region – taking our work to Panama. On my return from Cuba, I'd been asked to speak about my experiences at a rather posh event in Belgrave Square in London, talking to members of Canning House, an Anglo-South American pressure group. Indeed this day, 14 February, was the first time 'Third Man in Havana' had been unleashed onto an audience, which turned out to be somewhat bemused. It was comprised of ambassadors representing various South and Central American countries, British diplomats and Foreign Office staff, and several swarthy-looking businessmen wearing dark glasses, with well-groomed, glitzy women on their arms.

It wasn't a particularly romantic Valentine's Day for my wife, who was also in the audience, keen to find out what on earth we'd been doing in Cuba. In fact, I never feel very romantic on 14 February anyway, because my father Frank was born on that day in 1899 up in sunny Sunderland. It was he who introduced me to cricket at Grace Road, Leicester, in the early 1950s, when Leicestershire invariably came either bottom or next to bottom of the County Championship. Indeed they still do – *plus ça change,* and so on.

Despite the emotional connotations of the day, the talk went well, and even the Cuban ambassador, a stern supporter of the revolution, enjoyed it (or at least said he did, which is good enough for me). But perhaps the most surprising response to the talk was from an attractive young woman in the audience called Paola Ramirez, who worked at the Panamanian embassy. She had really enjoyed the talk, and wanted me to meet her boss, the Panamanian ambassador, who hadn't been able to make it, but who was a sports fanatic. She thought he might be persuaded to invite us to work in Panama.

5

PANAMA – A MAN. A PLAN.
A CANAL. PANAMA.

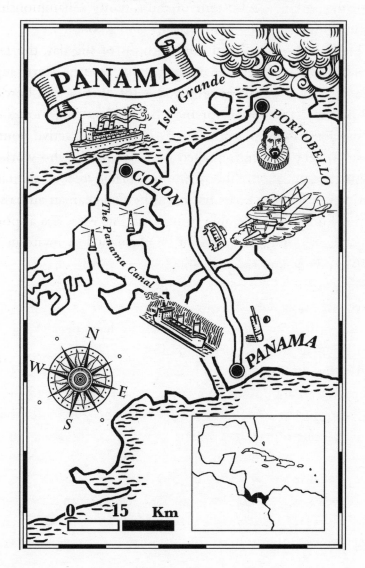

'P ALINDROME' IS ONE OF THOSE WORDS that we've heard but can never quite remember the meaning of. I've just looked it up again to make sure, and it's when a word, phrase or sentence reads the same if you turn it back to front. At school I used the phrase 'A Man. A Plan. A Canal. Panama.' to remember that, and this particular palindrome sums up the history of Panama over the past 150 years.

Ferdinand de Lesseps was the man, a Frenchman who had built the Suez Canal, but whose plan to build a canal across the isthmus of Panama foundered –he hadn't reckoned with malaria and yellow fever, which killed most of his workers. It was left to the Americans to finish the job, just before the First World War. Another man who had a plan in Panama was John Darwin, the 'canoe man' from Hartlepool who holed up there for a few years with a pile of fraudulent insurance money until he was found out. These two cases suggest that it's a country where dreams can be broken.

But our dreams of being able to work in Panama were not to be broken. This was entirely due to the work of the tireless Paola Ramirez, who I'd met at Canning House, and due also to the woman we were about to meet, Liliana Fernandez, the Panamanian ambassador to London.

Before our meeting with the ambassador, Paola briefed me with an added reason as to why she was so keen for us to work in Panama. It turned out that she was Colombian, and had been hired in London to work for the Panamanian embassy because she spoke perfect English as well as Spanish (and because she was very bright). But even though Panama is next to Colombia, she had had never been there, so a bonus for her was that she'd be able to accompany us as an interpreter. Because of all this, we were well prepared for our meeting with the ambassador, a very jolly lady who greeted us in impeccable English in her Panama flag-bedecked office in the heart of London's Mayfair. Most of the world's shipping is described as working under the 'Panamanian flag of convenience', so it was immediately clear how important the flag is to Panamanians.

Paola had found out that there was a long history of cricket in Panama. As in Cuba, successive waves of British Caribbean immigrants had settled in Panama as workers on projects all related to its location as the bridge between the Atlantic and the Pacific. The first wave helped the Americans build the railway linking the two oceans in the 1850s, the one that took prospectors to the Californian goldfields. The second wave came in De Lesseps' failed attempt to build his canal in the 1880s, and the third arrived to help the Americans complete the job in the early years of the 20th century. The first great West Indian cricketer, George Alfonso Headley, was born in Panama in 1909; his parents had been part of this wave of immigrant workers.

Added to this, apparently even before the canal was completed, British ships refuelling in Panama used to stop off and play cricket against the local Caribbean workers. Hindu and Muslim teams were also formed by other immigrants brought in to help with the work. As is often the case across the world, it was the descendants of these original South Asians who had kept the game alive in Panama throughout the 20th century, so much so that by 2002 the ICC awarded Panama affiliate member status, the same year that it awarded it to Cuba.

Paola presented all this cricketing background information with the confidence of a contributor to *Wisden* and, to use cricketing parlance, I was bowled over by her knowledge

– I hadn't been able to find anything like the information she'd dug out.

Just to show that I was concentrating, I thought I'd throw in the fact that I came from a long line of milliners in Leicester and that the famous Panama hat is also an essential accoutrement of the more conservative cricket watcher, but I was quickly corrected by Liliana, who said that Panama hats were actually made in Ecuador, and always had been. Paola stared across at me with a look that said 'Shut up you old fool.'

But we were able to chip in more sensibly with details of the work we'd been doing for years in London, and specifically the programmes in Jamaica and Cuba, which to my mind made for a comprehensive pitch. The ambassador seemed suitably impressed, and proceeded to demonstrate her sporting credentials by listing the Panamanian sporting greats.

Panama is another baseball-crazy country and one of the all-time great 'closer' pitchers in Major League baseball in the US is Mariano Rivera, who plays for the New York Yankees and is a proud Panamanian. And then there was Irving Saladino, who won Panama's first ever Olympic gold medal for the long jump at the 2008 Olympics. Still, although Liliana was a sports fan, and on our side, she needed convincing about cricket, a game she'd never actually seen.

It was May, early in the cricket season, and Middlesex were playing at Lord's, so I reckoned that the only way to close the deal was to take Liliana there to see the game at first hand, in the finest surroundings. It's always tricky taking foreigners to watch cricket for the first time. I've done it several times at Lord's with Israeli, French and Japanese clients keen to know about the game which they could tell dominated my life. I've had mixed results, but my guests have always been unanimous about the quality of the lunch.

I remember the story of the time: Donald Trelford, then the editor of the *Observer*, took another sports fanatic from the Americas to Lord's to introduce him to the game – Groucho Marx. Groucho was unusually quiet for most of the day, but clearly concentrating hard. This unnerved Trelford, and at the close of play he asked Groucho what he thought of it. 'Great,' he said. 'When does it start?'

But Liliana got the game straight away. She'd been to college in the US, knew loads about baseball, cricket's first cousin, and was soon discussing the intricacies of the LBW law like a *Test Match Special* summariser. Lunch in the Lord's Tavern cemented her understanding of the game's rituals, and she even stayed until the tea interval, such was her interest, although the idea of having tea so soon after lunch amused her.

Bill Bryson's wonderful book about Australia, *Down Under*, expands on this as he incredulously asks: 'What other day of top-class sport is interrupted by the players stopping to eat two full meals?' He's got a point, but the cricket tea in particular is surely one of the main reasons why we love the game so much.

Liliana wasn't just interested in the game itself, but also in what it could do for those on the fringes of society. Panama now owns and runs the canal itself, and is thus richer than a lot of its neighbouring countries, but there are still great inequalities, and Liliana was genuinely concerned that our work should concentrate on those suffering from some sort of disadvantage, particularly those with a disability. Although Liliana was a close relative of the president, as I gather is often the way in Panama, I still felt that she was talking not just as a top diplomat, but as someone genuinely concerned about her people, and also as a mother. This was a refreshing attitude, so we were keen to help her get what she wanted from our programme.

We shook hands on an agreement for the government of Panama to pay for our food and accommodation in Panama, and this, combined with free flights via New York from Dial a Flight, enabled us to pack our bags for Panama. But before then, as a thank you for her trip to Lord's, she invited us to an event in London, which she said would prepare us for our trip to Panama. It was a Salsa dance party being held by the embassies of Central America, and was as lively as it sounds. It whetted our appetite for a trip to a country not normally on the tourist map.

For a tiny country, Panama squeezes in a lot of history. Originally a province of Colombia until the Americans engineered its 'independence', the Panamanian city of Portobello on the Caribbean coast was once Spain's major port for the export of its South American empire's gold in the late 16th, 17th and 18th centuries. It was here, chasing this gold, that Sir Francis Drake's life came to an end in 1596, his body never found.

Well over a hundred years before the Spanish empire in the region collapsed in 1821, even the Scots had tried to found a colony there in Darien, finally giving up in 1700. By then most of the colonists had died, having spent a fortune of government money. This was a contributory factor in their 'merger' with England in 1707, a fact that Billy

Connolly often uses in his act, even though most Scots, no doubt including their First Minister Alex Salmond, probably don't want to remember it. It seems Europeans have never had it easy in Panama – the French there in De Lesseps' time found life so tough that the phrase '*Quel Panama*' became a synonym for a shambles.

Perhaps it's this maelstrom of history that attracted our friend Graham Greene to Panama, which he called 'a bizarre and beautiful little country'. Over several visits he became friendly with their president in the 1970s, General Torrijos, whose son was president at the time of our trip. Greene wrote a book about their relationship, *Getting to Know the General,* which I read while in Panama City. In 1979 General Torrijos negotiated with President Carter for the Americans to leave the Panama Canal Zone by the end of the century, which they did. He should have been regarded as a hero as a result, but in this part of the world it's easy to make enemies, and he died in a mysterious plane crash in 1981.

It seems that throughout history Panama has attracted all sorts of people – the Spanish, the Scots, the French, the West Indians and the Americans – and has then spat them back out. This did make me think that if all those fine peoples had found Panama difficult, what chance did we have of trying to establish disability cricket there?

Before the work in Panama City started, we visited the old city of Portobello where Sir Francis Drake had died, because Mikey particularly wanted to see the Cristo Negro, the black Christ, in Portobello's Iglesia de San Felipe. He – that's the black Christ, not Mikey – is a huge tourist attraction, and an icon to the minority black population in Panama. The church was packed with worshippers attracted by the lifesize statue of a Christ just like the representations you are used to seeing in churches, with one significant difference: the colour of his skin.

I'm not sure whether the visit to the church affected Mikey, but that evening staying nearby in a group of cabins on the Isla Grande, a small (not *grande* at all) island just off the coast, something very out of the ordinary and a little frightening happened. Mikey, as he later explained, was visited by the demons of his ancestors, and lay on his bed, screaming into the night.

This was the first time I'd ever witnessed anything like this, and it appeared that there was nothing we could do to penetrate Mikey's terrifying trance. We just had to wait until his ancestors had had their say, before Mikey came back to earth. Voodoo isn't as strong in Panama as it is in some other territories such as Haiti, but it seemed that this was an example of where Christianity meets the animist religions of black African ancestors, and who am I, as a desultory member of the Church of England, to deny it?

Talking of Mikey's ancestors, there had been a Jamaican presence in Panama for many years, and two of Jamaica's most revered sons and daughters had worked there. Mary Seacole, who later became famous for her work in the Crimean War – eclipsing the more 'establishment' Florence Nightingale – started to make her name as a nurse in the work camps of Panama in the 1850s, where death and disease were rampant.

A West Indian work song of the time summed up both the dangers of Panama and the reason why so many workers were still prepared to travel there:

Somebody's dying every day
I love you yes I do, you know it's true

And when you come to Panama how happy you will be
'Cause money down in Panama like apples on a tree

Another famous Jamaican who spent time in Panama as a journalist just before the First World War was Marcus Garvey, the founder of the Negro Improvement Association and an early proponent of the rights of black people. He died penniless in London in 1940, but, like Mary Seacole, is now an official Hero of Jamaica.

However, we were to learn of a Panamanian Jamaican even more of a hero to Mikey when we visited the Canal Museum in Panama City. The museum has an online archive of all those who helped build the canal, which we had a browse through because he thought he remembered his American cousins mentioning that one of their forbears had been in Panama. It didn't take Mikey long to find some Thompsons (spelt the Scottish way, as he always reminded us) and one with Christian names familiar to him. A call to the American cousins confirmed the news. Not only had Mikey's great-grandfather been in Panama, but he'd actually been born there.

It was a real 'Who do you think you are?' moment that affected us all, and which may in the end have explained Mikey's terrible night on the Isla Grande. Perhaps his great-grandfather was indeed trying to talk to him, when he had unwittingly come to visit him a hundred years on. For the duration of the trip, Mikey became 'Panama Mikey', wearing a fine, newly acquired Panama hat to confirm his newly acquired moniker.

The wonderfully efficient Paola had organised everything for us in Panama City. Especially a fabulous hotel in the smart La Boca area, overlooking the entrance to the canal, and bridged by the impressive 'Puente de las Americas', which links North to South America. It was at the hotel that we formally launched our programme, with a roomful of guests from the Panamanian government and their disability organisation, SENADIS, which was as impressive as any we'd come across anywhere.

SENADIS (translated) is short for the National Secretariat for the Social Integration of People with Disability. While this is a somewhat forbidding title, the organisation looks after the needs and aspirations of a surprisingly large proportion of the population. Panama is a small country, with only some 3.2 million souls, but 11.3 per cent of them have some form of disability, so it's a highly significant issue.

We were later told that there was an election in the offing, which is why the government was so keen to be seen to be helping this large number of people (voters). Still, we knew we could have an impact. Furthermore, if we could get things started properly, they would be more likely to be self-sustaining after the election had passed. So, like any good umpire, we were prepared to give them the benefit of the doubt, as so much effort had gone into the creation of the programme.

The programme had been given a name as grand as SENADIS; *Programa Criquet sin Barreras* (Cricket Without Boundaries), which was a neat way of summing up what we were trying to achieve. Government people love their speeches and the launch event was no exception. We hadn't really prepared any, but needed to do something, so we persuaded our rookie coach, on his first overseas trip, to sing the National Anthem, saying that it was the local custom to do so. This he duly did, extremely badly, to our huge amusement, and to the riotous applause of the gathered dignitaries.

We then demonstrated blind cricket, indoors, in the banqueting hall of the American-style Country Inn and Suites. Blind cricket always intrigues newcomers. To all intents and purposes it's normal cricket, apart from the bowler alerting the batsman that he's about to bowl, the ball being made of hard white plastic filled with ball bearings, so it can be heard, and the ball being delivered underarm. The wicket-keeper also has to have some sight, and therefore manages the game onfield.

Our blind coach led the demo and astounded all onlookers with his accurate bowling and deft batting, mainly sweeping the ball to leg, as is the way in one-day cricket. Back in England I'd opened the batting, sighted, against the England blind cricket team in a training match, and had been bowled second ball by an inswinging yorker delivered by their opening bowler. The only surprise was that I hadn't been bowled first ball, which had been just as good, but which I'd managed to keep out, more by luck than judgement.

Because our visit coincided with the rainy season, most of the work at our first venue was done indoors, in the sports centre at the Campo de Juego in the scruffy suburb of Bethania. This was an eye-opener into the 'real' Panama. Up until then, we'd been cosseted in the tourist areas and those set aside for the international businesses servicing the trade that passes through the canal. Bethania was more like Cuba, rundown and shabby, but happily also like Cuba in that it was full of young people anxious to learn about a new sport.

A lot of the coaches who'd turned up were disabled, too. For instance, Enoch and Rita were blind. One never really wants to ask about the individual circumstances of disability, but Rita was quite happy to share the story of how she became blind. She'd been in a tempestuous relationship, and her boyfriend had thrown acid in her face, which had blinded and disfigured her. Despite this horrific experience she was determined to get on with her life and help others come to terms with their disability.

Like the Cubans, the Panamanians very quickly picked up the game and enjoyed a full week's training, coaching and competition. The sports centre catered for all sorts of sport, all going on at the same time, and it was interesting seeing the interaction between our coaches and those specialising in baseball and boxing.

The baseball diamond was outside, and in between the downpours Mikey and the baseball coach of the Bethania team, a charismatic black guy named Enrique, shared their knowledge of throwing/fielding, pitching/bowling and hitting/batting. The parallels between the two are surprisingly strong and both learnt from each other. Much of the dramatic improvement in fielding in first-class cricket has come from cricket using techniques borrowed from baseball, indeed the Australian fielding coach is an ex-baseball player.

There are not so many parallels with boxing, however, and thank goodness for that. The boxing coach at Bethania was a wiry old guy called Ismael Laguna, another of Panama's sporting greats, who beat Carlos Ortiz for the world lightweight title in 1965, before losing it in 1971 to the Scottish boxer Ken Buchanan. Buchanan's no longer a household name, but my boxing friends tell me that until Joe Calzaghe he was probably Britain's best post-war boxer. Despite being beaten by Buchanan (twice), Laguna spoke endearingly about his opponent and said it had been a privilege to be in the ring with him. Boxing is obviously a violent sport, but this shows that it can still warrant its description as the 'noble art'.

Our work was easier in Panama than in Cuba, partly because of Paola, but also because we'd managed to get hold of a copy of *Tiempo de Juego* (Time to Play) a 60-page booklet produced by the ECB to introduce the game to young Spanish people. It had pretty much everything we needed in it, apart from the Spanish for 'third man'.

A wonderful festival finished our five days in Bethania, where more speeches were made and commemorative T-shirts handed out. The Bethanians watched as the Panamanian coaches took over our job and managed the whole event.

These programmes may run for only a few days and are often like the old TV programme *Challenge Anneka* – 'You've got three days to build a house', etc. – but it's amazing what can be achieved with willing local coaches and enthusiastic kids. Because we were able to take a back seat at this event we felt more confident that the programme would still have its own momentum after we had gone. The aim of our work is always to try to ensure that it can continue without us. The day was such a success that we decided to treat ourselves to a night on the town in Panama City, where Mikey wanted to sample the local reggaeton music and maybe some salsa too, as the ambassador had wonderfully demonstrated to us back in London.

The Baños Publicos club wasn't too good, maybe no surprise as it's the Spanish for 'public toilet', but the Platea was, although the bouncers had an issue with Paola as she, like everyone, had to show her passport, which was of course Colombian. Panamanians don't seem to have forgiven the Colombians for the time when they were in charge, and she was duly arrested, solely on the basis of her nationality, before we managed to get her freed with a display of British passport solidarity and reams of official-looking government paperwork. Despite Panama's outward impression of calmness, there are obviously big issues just below the surface, particularly drugs, which is why Paola's Colombian passport was of such interest to the police.

The second part of the programme took place in the old American Canal Zone, and thankfully the Americans had left behind all their facilities in good order, which, naturally, were fantastic. A pristine indoor basketball court provided a great venue for hundreds of local kids to get a taste of what cricket was like, and here the local Asian cricketers were on hand to help organise and coach.

Panama has a strong Asian community who have now been in the country for generations and are an important feature of the business scene. Being the rainy season we couldn't join them for a game outside, but they proudly showed us their cricket grounds, which were surprisingly good. Like the Cubans it was their ambition to become part of the Caribbean cricketing community – after all, Jamaica is closer to Panama than to Trinidad. Bearing in mind the keenness that we'd seen, this would seem to be a viable possibility, probably easier in Panama than in Cuba because of its relative wealth and greater exposure to the English language.

Of course, you can't leave Panama without a close look at the canal, so we said farewell to Panama with dinner at the Miraflore Locks restaurant, overlooking the massive locks.

There can be few more impressive sights — the giant container ships and glitzy cruise liners passed through the locks only yards away from our dinner table groaning with great Caribbean and Pacific seafood.

Just the other side of the locks you could see the vast building works underway to double the size of the canal to enable it to take even bigger ships. Every Panamanian we spoke to was very proud of this project, because it had been started after the Americans had ceded control of the canal. In fact, they all said that the canal was being better run by the Panamanians than by the Americans, which could well be true.

Mikey wondered whether his great-grandfather had actually helped build the old locks we were looking at, and we raised our glasses of fine Panama 'Alemana' lager to that poignant thought.

On the way back to Panama City we stopped off for another few beers and by chance met up with Toby Brocklehurst, whose late father Ben owned the *Cricketer* magazine for many years. We'd met Toby in Cuba, where he runs a travel agency. He was in Panama to expand his business there, in the expectation of direct flights being started from London.

We'd already talked about the possibility of Cuba being a tour destination for cricket teams from the UK, so now we thought, why not add Panama to the list? Teams could not only play cricket to a decent standard, but bring spare kit to donate, do some coaching and help further cement the game in this great little country. More than that, cricketers would learn about a place which, because of its position between North and South America, and between the Atlantic and the

Pacific, has been coveted by many empires, but which is now properly independent and defining its own destiny. Greene was right in describing Panama as 'a bizarre and beautiful little country' but he didn't see their enthusiasm for cricket, which to me makes it an even more endearing place.

There was a good postscript to our Panama programmes, back in London. Liliana Fernandez, the Panamanian ambassador, invited us back to the embassy to celebrate the success of our visit and to meet Dr Guillermo Moreno de Gracia, who was president of the Unión Latinoamericana de Ciegos (the Latin American Union for the Blind). He wanted Panama to lead in the spread of blind cricket across the whole of South America, a project maybe too big for us, but one which showed the power of the great game to captivate areas and peoples across the world where it might be least expected.

Another happy ending was in a post-meeting pub chat with one of our partners in London, the Metropolitan Police, when we discovered that they were very interested in how we'd been able to translate our work in London overseas. They wondered whether we could help them cement their relationship with the NYPD in New York by developing programmes relevant to their shared problems. This was about to create *another* exciting opportunity in *another* country apparently alien to cricket, but one, like Panama, with a long cricketing history.

6

NEW YORK! NEW YORK!

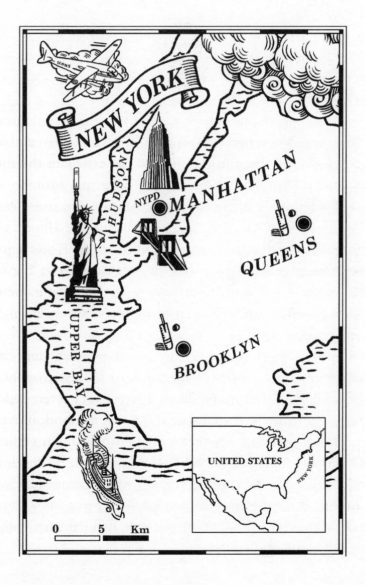

S O GOOD THEY NAMED IT TWICE. But despite New York being so good, it was my first visit since 1966, when I trained there to be a salesman for Vicks Vaporub and Lavoris mouthwash in Kansas, Missouri and Colorado. Despite the mundane nature of the products, I enjoyed it so much I planned to stay there, until the US Army asked me to go to Vietnam with them, an offer which I politely declined after I'd managed to scurry back to the UK. Because of that I'm always especially nervous going through US passport control, just in case they've still got my details on their system.

This time I was indeed detained by the authorities, but it was because my titanium hip had set off their alarm bells. A group of aged athletes with similar conditions were thus all corralled together to be interviewed with the usual rudeness by customs staff. We were easily the most unlikely bunch of suspected terrorists ever gathered together. From a draft dodger to a terror suspect in 45 years. All part of life's rich tapestry.

Going even further back in history was my meeting on our first evening in New York with a school friend I'd last seen in 1958 at the Buddy Holly concert in the De Montfort Hall, Leicester. Robin Lovell had moved to New York years ago and, still an avid Buddy Holly fan, had found me on the internet on the 50th anniversary of said concert. We had arranged to meet up 'when I was next in New York'. Robin said that memory should 'Not Fade Away' (sorry!), and it was wonderful to see him again, putting me in an immediately good mood for the work to come.

The New York cricket connection seemed an unlikely one, but the links between the West Indies and the US are very strong (there are many more West Indian expats in the US than the UK, for instance) and the US has also received waves of immigration from South Asia, just as in the UK. Added to this melting pot were the shared interest of the New York Police Department and London's Metropolitan Police in keeping their inner-city streets safe, and the blind governor of New York's policy of helping those with a disability in any way possible, making the idea of introducing tapeball cricket and blind cricket seem worth investigating.

The other main area for cricket in the US is the West coast, home to C. Aubrey Smith's famous Hollywood Cricket Club before the war. Some inner-city work using cricket had been done at the Compton Cricket Club in Los Angeles, who have even toured England. However, the game had not been used in this way on the East Coast, so it was pretty much a blank canvas.

Late 20th-century immigration has certainly reinvigorated cricket in the US, but as an ex-British colony, the history of cricket, especially on the eastern seaboard, is a long one. The New York Cricket Club, later called the St George's Cricket Club, was founded in 1838. The first international 'Test match' took place in 1844, and was between the US and Canada, a fact that all good pub quizzers know well. An England XI first toured the US in 1859, the team including such luminaries as the Johns Wisden and Lillywhite, as well as the wonderfully named Julius Caesar, who must have been getting on a bit by then.

The rise of more American sports, such as baseball, and the refusal of the Imperial Cricket Conference, the precursor of the International Cricket Conference (ICC), to allow the US into their cosy cartel signalled an inexorable decline in the game. The MCC staged a wonderful exhibition in 2010 comparing the respective histories of cricket and baseball and how they diverged – the accompanying book, *Swinging Away*, explains all.

To most Americans, 'cricket' is now just the name of a mobile phone company, but such things as the unexpected success of Joseph O'Neill's wonderful book *Netherland*, a story of post-9/11 New York centred around a group of ex-pat cricketers, have helped put the game on the map again, and no doubt will do so even more when the movie comes out.

'Minor nations' international cricket is now encouraged by the ICC, and a new purpose-built ground in South Florida has hosted the Sri Lankans and the New Zealanders playing one-day games. The format of these games – either 50-over or Twenty20 – is perhaps more suited to the Americans' legendary short attention span. Indeed, in early 2010 the IPL announced that it was planning to bring its 'fast food' version of the game to the land of fast food, although nothing has happened yet.

As icing on the cricketing cake, a Mr Dupaul Singh has opened Singh's Sporting Goods shop in Queens as the nation's first, and only, cricket store. The black and South Asian communities still live mainly in New York's poorer boroughs, and it was in Queens that we met the leaders of the USA Cricket Association for a conference to discuss the launch of a pilot blind cricket programme in New York, as well as a three-year plan to develop this version of the game across the US.

This all sounds very grand, but the venue, The Laresa Palace, 116-14 Rockaway Boulevard, South Ozone Park,

Queens, was a West Indian nightclub normally 'playing the best in reggae, soca and hip hop'. Nightclubs should never be seen during the day (the clue is in the name!) and the Laresa Palace was no exception. The excesses of the previous night's entertainment were all too evident, a heady mix of stale smells that it's best to gloss over.

Despite this, the conference started well, with a message of support read out from the blind governor of New York, James A. Paterson, who stated: 'As someone who has lived his entire life with a visual impairment, I know very well how important it is to empower those with disabilities. The promise of America is the promise that every person can participate fully and equally in our society. Blind cricket can help make that promise real for countless New Yorkers and Americans and I am proud to join with the hard-working individuals and organisations present in supporting this valuable endeavour.'

This was Governor Paterson's own Declaration of Independence, and every bit as powerful as the 1776 original, which famously states that: 'All men are created equal, that they are endowed by their Creator with unalienable rights, that among these are life, liberty and the pursuit of happiness.'

Fine words, but actually it was Governor Paterson's that made us puff out our chests and realise that perhaps we were about to achieve something important. If one doesn't suffer from a disability oneself, it's not easy to imagine the difficulties one encounters in doing a job, especially one as demanding as being the governor of a state, and it's remarkable that Governor Paterson has achieved so much despite this handicap.

I suppose the closest equivalent in the UK would be David Blunkett, who was in the cabinet of the Labour government for some years despite being blind. Interestingly, as a high-profile blind person, we approached him a few years back to help raise the profile of blind cricket, but he refused, saying 'I don't do blind.' I wouldn't criticise him for this attitude, as this was obviously his way of coping with his disability – just ignoring it.

The USA Cricket Association has had a chequered history, indeed it was suspended by the ICC as recently as 2007 for all sorts of misdemeanours. However, the newly reconstituted association comprised some impressive people, all of either Caribbean or South Asian origin, and all volunteers.

The chairman of the conference was Clifford Hinds – a good West Indian name – one of the USA Cricket Association's luminaries. His presentation of the three-year plan included the goal that the USA should become profi-cient enough to play in the Blind Cricket World Cup within those three years, an ambitious objective. Still, it was one which had already been achieved in the West Indies, so why not? After all, the USA is still the land of opportunity where anything can be achieved, despite recession and post-9/11 trauma.

The Blind Cricket World Cup mirrors its mainstream equivalent, and three have so far taken place, with teams from India, Pakistan, England, South Africa, Sri Lanka, Australia, New Zealand and more recently the West Indies taking part, the latter as a result of Mikey's work there. The other parallel with the mainstream competition is that England has never won it, but that's another story.

The conference rattled along at an impressive pace, and the assembled audience whooped and hollered their agreement to everything that was being proposed, with an enthusiasm normally reserved for revivalist prayer meetings (though such meetings don't normally take place in nightclubs). The efficiency of the meeting was wonderful to behold, but as the sound systems were being wheeled in at the end of the afternoon to transform the room back into a nightclub, we sussed one of the reasons why.

No matter, there was another good reason to finish on time, as food was ready at a local Guyanese restaurant where everyone decamped to celebrate a big day in the long history of American cricket.

The astonishing spread of the West Indian diaspora was brought home as Derrick Kallicharran introduced himself to us. Brother of Alvin, who played for Guyana, Warwickshire and the West Indies, Derrick had played club cricket in England before heading for the US to work in real estate. It was great to have him on hand to enthuse about the progress of American cricket, and to point us to the best items on the Guyanese menu, a subject which, I'm ashamed to say, seemed even more vital at that moment.

The media had been invited to the blind cricket demonstration at the New York Indoor Cricket School in the morning. We're used to the MCC Indoor School at Lord's, an impressive building overlooking the Nursery ground in leafy St John's Wood, home to Sir Paul McCartney and other multi-millionaires.

The New York Indoor Cricket School, however, was inside a converted warehouse on the corner of E 88th and Ditmus in Canarsie, Brooklyn (that's Ditmus, not Titmus like the late great Fred Titmus). It's surrounded by abandoned car parts from nearby auto shops and junk yards, and the entrance is concealed by seemingly abandoned tankers from 'Grease Monkey Inc., Free Oil Pick-Up'.

But inside was a hive of good cricketing activity. The US Twenty20 cricket squad, under their captain and mentor Steve Massiah, were practising ahead of their departure for Dubai for the world Twenty20 qualifiers. They looked good, and Steve was enthusiastic about their prospects, but in the end only Ireland and Afghanistan of the smaller nations got through to the finals that year. However, it's certainly true that one of the godsends of the Twenty20 format is that, although it dumbs down the game, it gives the smaller non-Test-playing nations a chance at the big time.

Without wishing to sound too blasé, our demonstration of blind cricket created the usual levels of astonishment that the game could be played at a good level by people with little or no eyesight.

Talking to Mikey and Tony over the years had educated me as to what playing blind cricket can do for someone who is visually impaired. The first thing it does is help develop trust in other people. When the batsman gets himself ready to face the bowler, he must trust the partially sighted opposition wicket-keeper, to help him position himself correctly at the wicket. And when the bowler says to the batsman

'Ready?' and the batsman answers 'Yes', the bowler has to trust the batsman not to move.

It's similar with field placings. There's nothing more annoying in mainstream cricket than when a fielder moves position without telling the captain. In blind cricket it's not just annoying, it's dangerous – if someone moves position it increases the possibility of collisions between fielders as they chase after the ball. The coach has a vital role in this, and must be able to guide the visually impaired players to their fielding positions. One of the roleplay activities used to introduce the game to potential coaches is to blindfold them and ask them to follow the leader of the session and to do whatever they say. And this isn't just on the pitch. It might be a trip upstairs to the balcony in the pavilion, or to where the toilets, showers, tea room and, most importantly, bar are. I've done it myself, and it's not easy – you have to trust your guide implicitly even if it feels counter-intuitive. Trust in all sport is important, but blind cricket takes this to a much higher level.

The other three characteristics that blind cricket helps develop – self-reliance, self-confidence and independence – are interlinked, and all increase over time as players get used to each other, to the game and to the coaches. A lot of young people with a disability are surrounded by a cocoon of safety provided by caring parents and friends. While this is under-standable, it can limit their chances to achieve things, and playing blind cricket can start to break down that cocoon and introduce more normality into their lives.

The pressure on coaches in all sport is immense, but blind cricket again takes that pressure to a new level, as it is up to the coaches to build on the trust invested in them by the players, to help them develop the confidence to be the best they can. I have watched Mikey and Tony transform the lives of many young (and not so young) people with visual impairments through the medium of cricket, using a combination of extreme patience, talent and good humour. Seeing this has been one of the most satisfying aspects of my involvement with these programmes. Even though I can't do the coaching myself, I can take some pleasure in having helped create the right environment for money to be raised to pay for it.

New York was no exception.

For instance Lloyd, originally from Guyana, had brought along his brother Colin, who had been recently blinded by diabetes, but who before that had played field hockey for the Guyanan national team. As a sportsman, he got the essence of the game in no time, as did all the other potential cricketers, which enabled the journalists to create a story. A full-page article appeared in the sports section of the *New York Daily News* the following weekend, under the headline 'High Hopes. Blind Cricketers Show Big Apple the Possibilities', which is exactly what Governor Paterson would have wanted.

The US Twenty20 team, good sportsmen to a man, stopped their practice to cheer us out as we left the New York Indoor Cricket School, and an old black guy who had been at the conference the day before thanked us for our work. He said he'd played cricket for years back in the West Indies before emigrating to the US. He had continued to play at New York cricket's very own 'Field of Dreams' – Marine Park, Brooklyn – but he'd never seen anything like blind cricket.

He didn't introduce himself but, for some reason, had brought along a brand new smart white shirt to give me – we were both about the same size. He said: 'I don't need no smart shirts anymore, but I'm sure you do.' I accepted it with an embarrassed thank you and gave him one of our 'New York' T-shirts. He then thrust a typewritten piece of paper into my hand and said, 'Read it later.'

I did, and under the heading 'Desiderato' (No, I don't know what it means either) was a homily to living a good life, ending with the phrase: 'You are a child of the universe, and no less than the trees and the stars you have a right to be here, but despite its sham, drudgery and broken dreams, it is still a beautiful world. Be careful. Strive to be happy.'

I guess it was a religious tract of some sort, and probably descriptive of the situation a lot of the recent immigrants find themselves in, but its positive ending sums up everything about Americans, from wherever they come. They are very open in their emotions and it was his way of saying thank you, just as Governor Paterson had done, much more formally, in his opening message to us.

The second part of our American mission involved a very different facet of the game, which had been trialled with success by Mikey on the streets of Hackney in inner-city London, with the help of the Metropolitan Police.

London had been traumatised by the 7/7 bombings almost as much as New York had been by 9/11. The attacks had been particularly poignant as they coincided with London being awarded the Olympics, and the follow-up failed attacks coincided with the Lord's Ashes Test. One of the responses of the Metropolitan Police had been to try to engage more with young Muslims 'at risk from radicalisation', and young people in general 'at risk of gun and knife crime', both of which are commonly used politically correct phrases that often hide some ugly truths.

We'd been working for a long time in the inner city with the sorts of young people who might fall into either or both of the two descriptions above, which led to Mikey's Hackney project being extended across London with the help of other partners(with the Met as the driving force). The projects are pretty simple: weekly sessions of tapeball cricket through-out the year, managed by young coaches who come from the inner-city communities themselves, and who therefore understand the problems and difficulties these young people face. Local police join in with these schemes and thus meet the young people in a non-confrontational setting, which is obviously unusual for both parties.

Trust develops over time, and early results have shown that less crime takes place among these groups. This isn't a cat-egorical answer to the problem, and as the 2011 riots have shown, there is much work still to be done, but frankly any progress in these areas where the same problems have fes-tered for a generation has to be good news.

Back across the Atlantic, received wisdom suggests that the New York Police Department has done a better job in reducing inner-city crime than the Met. Nevertheless, the latter's 'softly softly' approach in its cricket programmes had attracted plaudits on both sides of the pond. Whatever the differing results on the ground, there is no doubt that the NYPD has certainly done a better job than the Met in making a name for itself. The TV series *NYPD Blue* glamorised its work. Recent NYPD commissioners have become national heroes, while the Met's last two commissioners have met less positive fates. Everywhere you go in New York souvenir shops sell official NYPD merchandise such as beanie hats and T-shirts, proving that the US is as much the 'land of the brand' as 'the land of the free'.

I'd started to read Edward Conlon's book *Blue Blood* on the flight over. He's a serving officer in the NYPD whose book describing his experiences in the force became a *New York Times* bestseller. Its front cover says it's 'Beautiful and Imposing, Terrifying and Heartbreaking', and these were pretty much my emotions as we went through the many layers of armed security to get into NYPD's HQ , No. 1 Police Plaza, at the bottom of the Lower East Side by the Brooklyn Bridge.

No. 1 Police Plaza is New York's 'Gotham City' architecture at its most awe-inspiring. Big and brutal with no compromise, unlike, say, New Scotland Yard with its silly sculpture (complete with 'Making London a Safer Place' strapline) revolving outside. Dominating the NYPD's vast atrium is a memorial to all those hundreds of officers who have died in its service, each one named and dated, the longest list being on 11 September 2001.

That day is one of those 'I remember where I was' events. I was taking a pitch brief from the European Union intended to persuade wine buyers to specify natural Portuguese corks rather than more modern screw caps or plastic corks in wine bottles. It did strike me at the time that this was one of the daftest wastes of EU money I'd come across, which is saying something. We were earnestly informed that by supporting Portuguese cork – which they admitted has about a one in twenty chance of ruining your wine – we would protect valuable Portuguese jobs and cork oak forests. Well yes, but shouldn't the Portuguese just get their act together first? That was my only question, one which didn't go down well, and unsurprisingly we didn't get the job. Every cloud has a silver lining, however, and now I know the facts I always buy wine with screw caps. Knowledge is power, as the saying goes.

And then we heard the news of 9/11, an event from which, more than ten years later, repercussions are still being felt.

We were ushered into the office of the deputy inspector, a stocky man called Amin whose second name suggested a Muslim background. He summoned a sergeant, Ernesto, presumably a second-generation Italian, and a detective, Jeff Thompson, who had been deputed to head up the project. Shame he didn't spell his name Jeff Thomson, which would have been a neat coincidence with the great Australian fast bowler. The three of them summed up their city; a mixture of different ethnic backgrounds – Middle Eastern, Italian and Celtic – but united as proud New Yorkers. Our representative from the Met Police, who had done good work in getting the project off the ground in London, was only a police constable, and seemed all too aware that he was outranked.

We outlined what we'd done in London, which was enthusiastically received by Jeff, the detective, but less so by the other two, who were more quizzical, not being cricket aficionados. Jeff was – he had an Australian wife, and had been ribbed a lot about his name on trips to Oz, so knew about the game and liked it. He'd even founded the NYPD Cricket Club, which naturally had some very cool branded kit. I still enjoy wearing the cap he gave me as I lounge around on the boundary in Berkhamsted.

It seems that Jeff had been ploughing a lonely cricketing furrow engaging with the Caribbean and South Asian communities in New York, and that our arrival gave his putative projects much-needed credibility. We managed to get both Ernesto and Amin onside, and they were soon enthusiastically supporting the creation of projects in New York mirroring our work in London.

'I have the budget in place so I'll inform the commissioner that we start immediately,' said Amin, as he closed the hour-long meeting, shook hands and disappeared out of the room. I expected the *NYPD Blue* credits to start rolling and the music to come to a crescendo at that moment – the meeting had seemed like an episode of the show, with strong characters, a good story, and a successful ending. But that's just how they get things done in the good old US of A.

It seems that our visit had been as much of a catalyst as we'd hoped. New York's Finest made the announcement 'NYPD Youth Cricket Swings into Action' on their website. This was followed up by the *New York Daily News* and even by the *Sydney Morning Herald* in Australia (possibly confusing the

NYPD's Jeff Thompson with Sydney's own Jeff Thomson), who punned 'Bouncers in Brooklyn as NYPD pitches up Community Cricket'.

So our flying visit (thanks, British Airways) to the Big Apple had achieved what we had set out to do. Cricket in the US has had several false dawns, a bit like soccer, and will never replace the monoliths of American football, basketball, ice hockey and baseball. But there's a lot of cricket heritage there to be proud of, and the new Caribbean and South Asian communities are doing well in getting the game better organised so that, apart from community projects like these, it can also compete effectively in 50-over and Twenty20 cricket on a wider stage.

The possibility of the IPL coming to the US may be another false dawn, but it does demonstrate that cricket in the US is now on the global radar, and it would be terrific for the region's cricket if it did take off, in whatever format, because the US has so much more money than their close Caribbean neighbours, who are now struggling to compete with their 'first world' competitors.

But even if 'pro' cricket in the US doesn't happen, the largely ex-pat cricket communities there are very open to the different opportunities that fringe versions of the game – such as tapeball and blind cricket – can offer to help those on the edge of society. Such is the 'can-do' attitude in the US that the game in whatever form can only prosper and grow.

The ICC's 'Americas' region has certainly helped connect the US to the rest of the world cricket-wise, and as we discovered on our return to the UK, their 'Europe' region had been busy too. They'd heard about our work and wondered if we could help encourage their 'most enthusiastic member' Israel in some of the work they were planning. I'd worked in Israel a lot in my advertising career, have a lot of friends there, and it's a fascinating place. That was three good selfish reasons to go there, apart from any good we might be able to do using cricket.

7

ISRAEL – CROSS-BORDER CRICKET

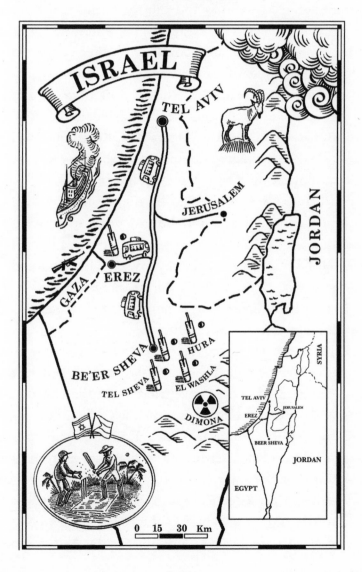

I WAS LOOKING FORWARD to going back to Israel. I first went there in the early 1980s to introduce local advertising people to the pleasures of commercial television advertising, which was just starting up there. I grew to love the place, as its history is our history. Its situation at the crossroads between Africa, Asia and Europe means that there are the remains of many civilisations to be found there. On top of that there is its crucial importance to three of the world's major religions: Judaism, Christianity and Islam.

Of course, the creation of the state of Israel in 1948 is still not accepted by all, and there are major ongoing problems in the region, but I will leave that discussion to others. There have been many attempts to establish peace, one of which followed the Oslo Peace Accord in 1993. Following that agreement, I was asked to be responsible for advertising Israel in the UK as a jolly holiday destination. We came up with a television campaign based around the line 'Hav'a Great Holiday in Israel' to the tune of the Hebrew folk song 'Hav'a Nagila'. Our Jewish creative director hated it, but the Israeli clients loved it, as it portrayed their beautiful and interesting country as a peaceful place.

In the search for peace, particularly among the younger generation who might be seen as less entrenched in their views, many good people have tried to get the two populations, Arab and Jew, engaging with each other. Perhaps the most successful attempt has been Daniel Barenboim and the late Edward Said's setting up of the West-Eastern Divan Orchestra. This is comprised of 40 per cent Jews, 40 per cent Arabs and 20 per cent Europeans, and has even played in Gaza, much to the annoyance of the Israeli government. On that occasion Barenboim, a Jew born in Tel Aviv, famously declared 'I am a Palestinian,' which, geographically speaking, is true. He also said, wisely: 'People have got to learn to live side by side, not back to back.'

Sport has also tried to engage with the issue in a similar way, with some success, especially in basketball and football, where Arabs and Jews play side by side in professional teams. But despite this there is still very little interaction between the two communities.

The ICC is surprisingly keen to use cricket to help disparate groups come together, indeed their mission statement is 'To captivate and inspire people of every age, gender, background and ability while building bridges between continents, countries and communities.' Often such statements are mere window dressing, but it was at the ICC's request that we landed in Tel Aviv to scope out the possibility of using cricket to help build such bridges.

This would be easily our most challenging task to date, partly because of the inherent political problems in Israel and because the mutual suspicions between the races and religions run so deep, but also because we expected knowledge of cricket in Israel to be very much less than in some of the other countries where we had operated. But the ECC (the European bit of the ICC) said there was a good guy down there who'd started to work across the communities and who wanted some help in setting up programmes.

That good guy was George, who met us at Tel Aviv airport. He is Israel's cricket development officer (yes, they've got one) and was as far from any Israeli stereotype as it's possible to be. For a start he was from Scarborough, Yorkshire. What a fine cricketing place to come from. Scarborough summed up everything that was good about cricket in the heady days of the 1950s, when the game was all about festivals and fun, rather than fitness and focus as it is today.

George isn't Jewish by birth, but like a lot of young men his age he took himself off to a kibbutz in Israel in the 1970s because it was sunny, not too far away and didn't cost much. Nowadays, similar young men can go all over the world on gap years which are really no more than extended holidays. Many come back claiming that it's changed their lives, but apart from the suntan and some dodgy new mates in Thailand, it usually hasn't.

George had aimed to come back home too. He'd trained as a pastry chef, for which there was good work to be found in the hotels of Scarborough, but two things happened to keep him in Israel. First, he fell in love with a beautiful young Jewish girl from Iraq, whose family had just arrived as refugees from Baghdad, and second he discovered that there was a big demand for cakes in Israel.

I know it's a cliché, but Jewish people love their cakes, a love brought to Israel by the Ashkenazi Jews from Central Europe. With the country starting to prosper, hotels were springing up in Tel Aviv and Eilat encouraging even more cake consumption, not just for the burgeoning holiday market, but for the constant round of barmitzvahs, weddings and funerals. George's skills were just what they needed.

He'd been a cricket man in Scarborough – I guess you had to be in those days – but that was far from his mind when, after a few years of marriage and with a young family, George decided to take the plunge and accept the offer to decamp to the fast-expanding town of Be'er Sheva in the Negev Desert. There he found that cheap new housing was available for the thousands of immigrants pouring into post-1973 Israel. This was a time full of optimism, when Israel, with its newly won territory and confidence was bossing the Middle East. How things change.

It was hard work, but George's new bakery did well in Be'er Sheva and he was soon able to expand and hire staff, including local Bedouin Arabs who had adopted a more settled lifestyle. With the demands from his family diminishing as they grew older, George now had enough time to indulge his childhood passion – cricket.

Unlikely as it might sound, there had been cricket in Be'er Sheva for a while. Certainly British and Australian troops played there in 1917, as Allenby and Lawrence (of Arabia) planned their attacks on Turkish strongholds on their way to conquering Jerusalem. Cricket carried on in the inter-war years of the British Palestinian mandate, but was regarded, a bit like in Ireland, as a 'garrison' sport, played by the colonial power.

The real cricketing impetus in Be'er Sheva came with the arrival of Indian Jews to the area in the 1960s. There had been a large community of 'Baghdadi' Jews in Bombay since the 18th century and, as I'd discovered when touring India, they joined the other religious groups there in playing cricket. So, as soon as the Indian Jews arrived in Be'er Sheva, they started a cricket club, built a rudimentary ground and linked up with other clubs across Israel, which were made up of South African, Australian and English Jewish immigrant players. A flourishing cricket league was created.

Although the sport is still small in Israel, these immigrants obviously have clout, because if you pick up a copy of the *Jerusalem Post* (the English language daily newspaper which used to be owned by Robert Maxwell) the cricket scores, both at home and abroad, are there to savour – worth the few shekels cover price on their own.

Two of the leading lights in Israeli cricket, to whom we were introduced by George, were Stanley Perlman, a South African, and Naor Gudkar, an Indian, who were chairman and CEO respectively of the Israel Cricket Association, having been cricketing pioneers in the 1970s. Stanley has a nice line about the history of cricket in Israel: 'Israel is the land of milk and honey, the land of miracles – and the survival of cricket in Israel *is* a miracle.'

In 1974, Israel became an associate member of the ICC, with only Pakistan objecting – perhaps understandably so soon after the 1973 Yom Kippur war, not that Israel started it. Another fact illustrating the madness of Israel's modern history is that as well as a war in 1973, that year also saw cricket become a Jewish Olympic sport for the first time. The Maccabi Jewish Olympics take place every four years, with teams from all over the world taking part. Indeed, an old client of mine, Mark Cohen, who played a bit for Middlesex seconds, captained the Irish Jewish team at the games in the 1990s. It's such a shame that the 2012 Olympics in London isn't featuring cricket. Twenty20 would be the perfect format, with all the facilities already there, and it would be a fantastic showcase for the game.

A recent Israeli movie called *Turn Left at the End of the World* tells the story of a group of young Indian Jewish settlers arriving in Be'er Sheva in the 1960s. They are astonished by the barrenness of the place, concerned about the racial prejudice they are facing, but most of all worried about where they are going to play cricket. It's Naor Gudkar's favourite film.

As George drove our minibus south from Tel Aviv on the motorway, the coastal plain gave way to the Negev Desert, which does indeed look like the end of the world. Road signs to nice places like Jaffa and the Dead Sea gave way to less alluring ones like Dimona, the site of Israel's main nuclear facility. You approach at your peril – Mordechai Vanunu was jailed by the Israelis for eighteen years in 1986 for giving away some of its secrets. A less notorious son of Dimona is Yossi Benayoun, the Chelsea footballer, whose nickname is 'The Diamond from Diimona'.

But if Dimona is notorious, Erez, the main crossing point into the Gaza Strip is even more so. We asked George to take a small detour off the main road so that we could have a look at the Erez crossing. It was only weeks after the last confrontation between Hamas and the Israel Defence Force, when Israeli patience ran out following hundreds of rocket attacks from the Gaza Strip on Israeli towns such as Ashdod and Be'er Sheva. They retaliated with arguably disproportionate force and destroyed huge swathes of the already ramshackle towns and villages in the Gaza Strip. Most ordinary Israelis are not political. They want what everyone wants – a peaceful prosperous country in which to bring up their children.

Only three months prior to our visit, Hamas had started firing BM-21 Grad rockets from Gaza, bringing Be'er Sheva within their 25-mile range. One rocket landed next to the Be'er Sheva Cricket Club pavilion, just on the boundary of the sandy ground, which of course greatly upset George. It did little damage, which is hardly surprising since the Be'er Sheva Cricket Club pavilion is a converted nuclear bomb shelter, which descends two storeys down into the desert. Following this attack, the pavilion was requisitioned by the Israel Defence Force. This upset George even more because it meant cancelling that weekend's cricket fixtures, but he did admit that the previous few weeks' bombardment had affected his bowling. 'How can you possibly concentrate on your line and length when there is a threat of a rocket attack?'

Because Israelis face the possibility of attack every day of their lives, they have to look at the funny side of their situation. I guess it was the same in the Blitz in London in 1940 when the indomitable cockney spirit helped see us through those dark days. George wasn't keen to approach the Erez crossing, but agreed because we wanted to take photos. Rather thoughtlessly, in retrospect, we then decided to have an impromptu game of tapeball cricket.

We started to play about 100m from the heavily fortified crossing, with walls, trenches, barbed wire, barking guard dogs and nervous young Israeli troops surveying the scene from the safe vantage point of their lookout posts. A desolate place. A frightening place. I'd been in Israel during the first Lebanon war in the early 1980s, and had gone to the front on the Golan Heights where Israeli artillery was firing into Syria, but this was much worse. Whereas the Golan Heights are attractive wooded hills, this is flat, barren, flyblown and eerily quiet, apart from the guard dogs. No one in their right mind goes to Erez without good reason.

I was as nervous as the watching Israeli soldiers and bowled an over, from the Gaza end, which was about as scruffy as the surrounding desert. The last of the resultant sixes went right over the Israeli defences into the Gaza Strip. We were just about to ask 'Can we have our ball back please?' when an Israeli armoured personnel carrier came careering round the corner in a cloud of dust, and screeched to a halt about where cover point should have been. Cover point had moved back to the boundary after the first two balls of my over. About half a dozen heavily armed Israeli troops leapt off their vehicle and cocked their rifles. The platoon commander ran up to George, who had already started to walk towards them, and started screaming at him in Hebrew.

We clambered back onto the bus a touch shamefaced, particularly as poor George had obviously taken the rap for us. After we'd got back onto the main road he seemed calm enough, so I tentatively asked him what the officer had said. 'Not much,' George answered. 'Just that he thought that your bowling was shit.'

The Gaza situation is desperate, and hard to understand for an outsider, but there's a wonderful series of crime books by Matt Rees, who's worked in Israel for years. They feature a Palestinian detective called Omar Yussef, and one of them, *The Saladin Murders*, is set in Gaza. This provides a good insight into what life is like there for the ordinary people caught up in the conflict.

We settled into rooms in the middle of Be'er Sheva at the University of the Negev, founded by Israel's first president — Ben Gurion. Ben Gurion came from the Negev and set the new nation on a self-help, socialist (with a small s), kibbutz-led course which worked well, and set a suitably ascetic example himself.

Be'er Sheva comes as a bit of a shock after the emptiness of the desert. It's an expanding, modern city of around 200,000 Jewish Israelis, full of dual carriageway roads, sprawling identikit housing, and shopping malls. A bit like Milton Keynes, except that Milton Keynes isn't surrounded by a desert where over 100,000 Bedouin Arabs live in tiny settlements, or at least it wasn't the last time I went there.

Emphasising the tempestuous history of the region, right outside the university was a large Commonwealth War Graves cemetery containing the graves of hundreds of mainly Welsh and Australian soldiers. They were killed in the last ever British mounted infantry charge at the Battle of Be'er Sheva in 1917. There's a similar cemetery in the middle of Gaza, sadly not kept as immaculately as that in Be'er Sheva.

Most of the British troops who fought at the battles of Gaza and Be'er Sheva were from mounted infantry yeomanry regiments. My father was in the Leicestershire Yeomanry as a teenager and served in the First World War. His records have been lost, but my uncle George served in Palestine and I remember him telling me that it was regarded as a cushy posting compared to the trenches in France. It didn't seem that cushy to me as I surveyed row upon row of white gravestones.

Among the graves of the now-forgotten heroes is that of Tibby Cotter, an Australian mounted infantryman who before the First World War played 21 Tests for Australia and who was reckoned by many to be the fastest bowler in the world, earning him the nickname 'Terror' Cotter. Get it?

Unlike many Australians he'd survived Gallipoli, but on 31 October 1917, when the 4th Australian Light Horse Brigade was capturing Be'er Sheva, Cotter, a stretcher bearer, was shot dead at close range by a Turkish soldier. The official history states that 'he behaved in action as a man without fear' as he made the supreme sacrifice.

I don't expect many people have visited Cotter's grave, but I did, and instead of a red rose I left a red cricket ball for him. I know about Cotter only because for years I owned a painting of him by Gerry Wright from his 'Cricket's Golden Summer' series. I sold it after a few years because it was so sad, with him staring empty-eyed out of the picture surrounded by a field of poppies, representing death. I'm pleased to say that the painting now has a much better home in the wonderful museum at the Melbourne Cricket Ground.

The drive out to Hura, a Bedouin Arab village only five miles or so out of Be'er Sheva, was unremarkable, but in those five miles one also seemed to travel decades back in time, to a down-at-heel settlement of half-built houses, beaten-up old cars, donkey carts and meandering goats, all amid a forest of mosques.

There are over a million Bedouin Arabs living peaceably within Israel. Although they are Israeli citizens, it's obvious that they don't have access to many of the privileges of Israeli Jews, hence the endemic problems between the two groups. George said that Hura was one of the better Bedouin villages, but above many of the houses flew the green Hamas flag, and only a week before a sixteen-year-old girl from the village had been shot dead by the police, after she fired at an Israeli security base on the outskirts of Be'er Sheva.

We met Abu Hamed outside Hura's Almadjad middle school. Both the school and Abu Hamed defied the norms of the Bedouin Arab situation. The school was newly built in Jerusalem stone by the Negev Israeli Council, and Abu Hamed was smartly dressed in Western clothing as he climbed out of his shiny Mitsubishi 4×4. George had been working with Abu Hamed for a while, despite the fact that direct contact is generally not encouraged between Arab and Jew. Hamed was the sports coordinator for the area and the two got on well – George brooks no prejudice. Abu Hamed's fluent Hebrew meant that we could talk to him via George, to see if the school would allow us to introduce cricket to their pupils.

We were ushered into the headmaster's office and joined by the school's PE teacher. To me headmasters' offices are always daunting places, a bit like dentists' surgeries. As I sat there, I went back to the winter of 1963, remembering a visit to the Oakham School headmaster's office with my parents, which ended with my expulsion. Another story, maybe best forgotten.

This meeting wasn't looking too good, either. The headmaster, Kamel Abu Elkiyan, was grim-faced, although we got a smile out of his secretary, who poured us traditional Bedouin mint tea and offered us sweetmeats. Our tortuous English-to-Hebrew-to-Arab presentation of what we wanted to do and why seemed to be falling upon stony ground, but I could sense a glimmer of interest from the PE teacher, Omar Abu Alhadja, so concentrated my powers of persuasion, such as they are, on him.

After we'd finished, we, and George, were asked to leave the room. From outside the door we could hear voices in discussion that were, at least, not as aggressive as those of the Israeli soldiers at the Erez crossing. Eventually the PE teacher came out with a grin on his face which even I, with no Arabic (or Hebrew for that matter), knew was a result. However, the headmaster wanted to see what this tapeball cricket business was all about, and demanded an immediate demonstration from us, to be played out in front of the whole school.

No pressure then! Following my disastrous bowling at the Erez crossing, I was concerned that I would let the side down. No worries, mate. As it turned out, line and length came back a treat, and after only ten minutes the children, both boys and girls, were demanding to play. Permission was given by the headmaster — whose stony face had softened to impassive — and play started. First the boys, as is the way in Muslim cultures, and then the girls.

They loved it, and got it straight away. Abu Hamed took instruction from George, and Abu Hamed gave instruction to the PE teacher. But the kids didn't seem to need it. There were a few dodgy bowling actions, certainly, but nothing as dodgy as Muralitharan and Malinga, as well as some batting which Boycott would have hated, but Botham would have loved.

At the end of the lesson, we organised an impromptu batting competition between the boys, which was narrowly won by Nadji Mahmed Abu Shuldrum, who scored 11 runs, versus Doa Musa Alsayed's 10. A lot to write into the scorebook there. We left a pile of kit for them to use and said that God and Allah-willing we would see them the following week, when they would be playing against young Jewish children of the same age in Be'er Sheva.

It might seem to be a simple thing to organise tournaments between groups of local schoolchildren, but in Israel nothing is simple. George had done a brilliant job in getting his local Jewish children involved, but even though George and Abu Hamed had excellent personal and working relationships, the history between the two communities still prohibited direct contact with the Arab children.

Most forward-thinking Israelis want a more normalised relationship with the Arabs, especially with the Bedouin Arabs, and Amos Oz, arguably Israel's finest living writer, has fought for this. But there are hard-liners, particularly among religious and Russian Jews, who are opposed to compromise and unfortunately their votes count. Oddly enough, the fact that we were English – and not just white English but black English too, since Mikey was with us – rendered us neutral in the Arab/Jewish struggle, which made our involvement 'kosher', so to speak.

If only diplomacy were as simple there would be no problematic issues between countries and peoples. At least in a tiny way our experience was demonstrating the power of sport, and in particular cricket, to do good.

With the excitement of Hura still ringing in our ears, Hamed suggested we visit another Bedouin village a few miles away. This was El Washla, and it was very different from Hura. A lot of Bedouin villages are not officially recognised by the government of Israel, partly because they are somewhat fluid settlements and partly because the Israelis want the land for housing, agriculture and forestry.

After a long battle, El Washla had finally been recognised by the state, although it had no running water, electricity or roads. Hamed's 4×4 came in useful negotiating the miles of off-road track that led to the group of huts, tents and animal compounds which was the village. We were met by the sheikh, the council head and the elders, resplend- ent in their tribal clothes. Hamed said we were the first foreigners they'd ever met, and they wanted to make us welcome.

Lunch of chicken and rice had been prepared for us, together with bitter coffee and sweet tea. We sat on the ground, and ate with our fingers, just like our hosts, prop- ping ourselves up with cushions laid out on rugs. Across the Middle East there are tourist excursions to eat 'Bedouin style', but this was the real thing, and we felt very honoured. Mikey got so comfortable after lunch that he fell asleep, which amused our hosts as he started to snore like a Co-op horse. They'd never seen anyone as big as him before, or as black, for that matter and when he woke up they insisted on dressing him up as an Arab sheikh, Lawrence of Arabia-style which provoked much merriment for all.

Hamed suggested to the elders that maybe the children of the village might like a game of cricket. This took some explaining, which was followed by a lot of heated discus- sion. Mikey said they must be talking about Duckworth/ Lewis, although apparently the cricket debate was actually interspersed with another one about the falling price of goat hides. But in the end they said yes, so we plonked our kit on the village football pitch, which was only vaguely flat and had only one goal, and waited for the village children to arrive. One by one, they did.

We didn't do much more than just hitting the ball, as we had another school to visit, but the kids enjoyed it, although the field placing was 'Bedouin style' – mid-off would wander over to the covers, and long leg to third man. I always get ratty when fielders move from where they're meant to be, but we didn't make a fuss, as wandering about is very much in the Bedouin blood, and who were we to complain, having been so royally entertained?

The final Bedouin visit was to a girls' school in the village of Tel Sheva. Hamed said the girls didn't want to miss out on the opportunity to try a new sport, and, as at Hura, the whole school turned out to watch a demonstration and then to play themselves. While all the girls were correctly dressed according to Muslim custom, it didn't stop them running just as much as the boys, and smacking the ball all over the place. It's difficult coaching when you're not allowed to touch the pupils, but the local teachers soon grasped the game and took over. Again, we left a pile of kit behind and said that we looked forward to seeing them in Be'er Sheva.

George had already been coaching in the Jewish schools in Be'er Sheva, but particularly wanted Mikey to visit a school in one of the new areas of town where there was a high proportion of Ethiopian Jews – the Falashas, or black Jews of Israel, who were controversially spirited out of Ethiopia in the 1980s and 1990s. About 10,000 Falashas and their descendants live in Be'er Sheva, and suffer from discrimination because of their 'difference' and their difficulty in absorbing Hebrew.

So Mikey and I turned up at the Afiq school, which had a fair number of Falasha pupils, to offer some moral support and introduce them to cricket. We arrived on Holocaust Day, a day of sirens, silence and celebration to mark the end of the holocaust. Sirens across town signalled the start of the silence, which was immaculately observed by all the children. Neither Mikey nor I are Jewish, but we immediately felt at one with everyone in marking the event which had been the catalyst for the creation of the state of Israel.

After the silence came the celebration, as the pupils performed a series of playlets and dances and showed off artwork they had created to mark the day. It seemed trite after this show of emotion to demonstrate cricket, but the teachers were keen, and the Falashas particularly wanted to see Mikey in action, and to touch him, as someone who also had African roots. Mikey in action was an awesome sight that day, as he didn't just do cricket – he sang songs, and performed an impromptu 'Falasha Rap', which all enjoyed even if they didn't understand a word of it.

On competition day in Be'er Sheva everyone was nervous. A hundred or so Bedouin Arab children were coming to town, from four Bedouin villages – Hura, Tel Sheva, Lakia and Keseifa. The British Foreign Office was coming down, as well as the world's media, well, BBC TV and Reuters, anyway.

The Foreign Office in London had been helpful in smoothing our path to Israel, and they like to know what any visiting Brits are up to, as it is such a combustible area. Before our visit I'd popped in to see Edward Roman for a briefing. He introduced himself as 'Israel Desk Officer and middle-order Foreign Office batsman', which was a good start. We talked briefly about the situation in Israel, which he described as 'a bit volatile on the border' – something of an understatement, since hundreds of Palestinians had recently died in the Gaza Strip following the Israeli bombardment, as well as some Israelis in the Hamas rocket attacks that had prompted it.

We talked a lot more about cricket, and he loved the idea of what we were trying to achieve. He said that the British ambassador in Tel Aviv was also a cricket man and described him as 'a decent chap, and a reasonable wicket-keeper'. To be honest, I always worry a bit about wicket-keepers. Strange, impish, solitary figures, never far away from catching 'Jack Russell Syndrome', a medical condition too troubling to go into in detail here.

The British embassy had alerted the BBC and Reuters because they knew that both local correspondents were cricket lovers, and the embassy had sent down a junior diplomat from Tel Aviv as they were always looking for 'good news' stories in a region very short of them.

The competition took place at the Keidar Centre at Kaye College, Be'er Sheva, a teacher training college dedicated to trying to break down barriers between Arab and Jew. The principal of the centre, Dr Riva Levenchuck, was proud to be involved in another groundbreaking scheme to help achieve this aim. But she was still nervous because of the attack the previous week, and because of the sheer quantity of Bedouin children arriving. Even though you can see the outskirts of Be'er Sheva from, say, the hilltop village of Hura, most children there had never been there, such was the separation between the communities.

The Bedouin pupils were split up into teams of six and asked to line up against the Jewish opposition. Team names were chosen which didn't indicate where they were from, to minimise any tribalism, so there were names like the Snakes, the Lizards, the Camels and the Lions.

Each said who they were, shook each other's hand and wished each other good luck.

Tears welled up in my eyes and I'm sure they did in those of most adults watching, whether they were Jew, Arab or Gentile. I've been going to Israel for over 30 years and have seen the situation deteriorate year-on-year. If only adults could be like these children there would be no problems.

For over two hours the children played good cricket, in spite of the desert heat and the fact that most had been playing the game for only a week. Girls and boys. Arabs and Jews. Nobody really bothered about who won or lost; they were just there for fun, for a runaround, for a laugh. We gave prizes for the best Jewish team and the best Arab team, which seemed a sensible way to finish without starting another Arab-Israeli conflict, and individual stars were lauded too.

We talked to some of the children. Osher and Ilana, both from Be'er Sheva, said it had been a lot of fun, and Abdulla, an eleven-year-old from Hura who had never been to Be'er Sheva before, said: 'You know, I felt really good, because I felt I was playing with good people.' Such a simple sentiment, but one which, if multiplied over and over and over, might just get the country on the road to peace.

George was ashamed of himself because he cried – 'People from Scarborough don't cry, your tears freeze on your face,' he said. But this project had worked because of him and Hamed, two men dedicated to trying to make Israel – the whole of Israel

– a better place. Seeing them hug each other as certificates were given out to all the kids is something I'll never forget.

Our British diplomat friend loved the day. Having been brought up in Northern Ireland, he knew a lot about sectarian strife, and wished something like this had been tried in Belfast in the 1970s and 1980s.

The BBC man was also overwhelmed. He'd been born close to Edgbaston, so knew his cricket, but as the BBC man in the Middle East he'd been away from the game for a while. He interviewed everyone, and his piece led Sunday morning's BBC TV news that week back home. He said only months before he had been the only Western journalist reporting from inside the Gaza Strip, under attack from Israeli forces, and that in his three years in Israel as Middle East correspondent he'd never filed a good news story from the country – this was his first one. That's the power of the game, which has such inner strength that it can attack even intractable issues such as the Arab/Israeli divide.

The story was picked up across the world. A friend of mine on holiday in New Zealand saw it in the Auckland papers. Michael Atherton featured it in a wide-ranging article under the headline 'When the Ball Replaces the Bullet'. Duncan Campbell in the *Guardian* wrote 'Cricket Drive on the Stickiest of Wickets Aims to Unite Israeli Arabs and Jews', and even the *Jewish Chronicle* in London lauded the fact that 'Israeli and Arab kids team up for cricket'.

Good news travels fast, as the saying goes.

The ICC had made the introduction between us and George, and just let us get on with it as best we could, but they were astonished at the results. So much so that in 2009 'Cross Border Cricket' won both the European and Global award for the best Cricket Development Programme in the 'Spirit of Cricket' category, a fact of which George, Stanley, Naor and all at the Israel Cricket Association can be very proud.

Despite the political situation between Arab and Jew remaining consistently difficult, George's work continues apace and his programme has been extended to other Bedouin Arab villages around Be'er Sheva, such as Tel Sheva and the settlement of the Al Sayed tribe. The intention is to eventually take the work up to Jerusalem, which is very much the 'fault line' in Arab/Israeli politics.

The tremendous publicity and plaudits achieved by this work were of great interest to the ICC, who, true to their word of 'building bridges between continents, countries and communities' suggested that maybe work like this might be of help in Sri Lanka, a country much more soaked in cricket, but also suffering from the results of years of war and tension between the two major communities, the Tamils/Hindus and the Singhalese/Buddhists.

8

SRI LANKA – WHERE CRICKET IS LIFE

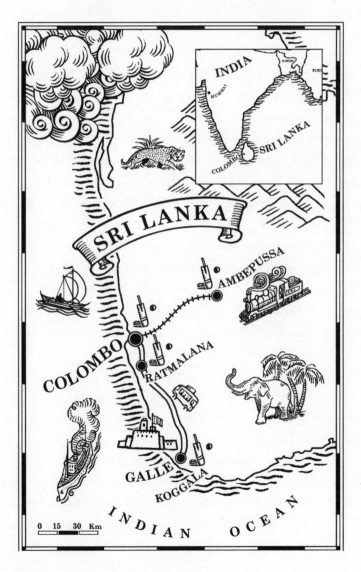

BEING ASKED TO HELP rebuild the lives of children in Sri Lanka as a result of our successes elsewhere was yet another big challenge. Not only had these children had to cope with the terrible tsunami which had caused such devastation, but the civil war too had cost thousands of lives and left many homeless and orphaned. This was a chance to see if cricket could help those who had lost everything.

And yet it wasn't always thus. The devastation that befell Sri Lanka in the late 20th and early 21st centuries through a killing combination of man-made and natural disasters is in sharp contrast to its much more peaceful and placid past. Marco Polo called it 'the finest island of its size in the world', and when visiting Sri Lanka Gandhi said that 'the natural scenery I see around me is probably unsurpassed on the face of the earth'. Sri Lanka, or Ceylon, as it was previously called, has attracted rave reviews throughout history.

Over the centuries its beauty and natural resources attracted many adventurers to the island, including three colonial powers – the Portuguese, the Dutch and the British. This colonial polyglot melting pot prompted George Bernard Shaw to say: 'I was convinced that Ceylon is the cradle of the human race because everybody there looks an original. All other nations are obviously mass produced.'

Its reputation in the cricketing world has always been as a place that, like its near neighbour India, is cricket crackers. Sir Pelham Warner imperiously stated in the 1920s, 'There is no finer place in the British Empire where cricket is played more enthusiastically and in a finer spirit than Ceylon.'

The British Empire is obviously the historical reason for this, as generations of British colonial administrators and tea planters — the latter including Sir Colin Cowdrey's father — developed the game and passed on their enthusiasm. Many Ceylonese players used to come to England to ply their trade, and at Leicestershire's Grace Road, Clive Inman and Stanley Jayasinghe are fondly remembered by myself and other old codgers from the 1960s.

At the other end of the professional cricketing spectrum, English and Australian Test teams used to break their long sea voyages with games in Colombo, the capital, although it took until 1981 for Sri Lanka to be accepted as a Test nation. That should have presaged a happy future, but sadly from then on Sri Lanka began to suffer, first from the 30-year Tamil/Singhalese civil war, which cost over 100,000 lives, and then from the 2004 Boxing Day tsunami which took 30,000 lives. For such a seemingly joyful place and people, it's also a sad fact that the suicide bomb, now such a common feature on the news, was invented in Sri Lanka.

It has been said that perhaps only cricket has kept the country together through these difficult times. Against all the odds, Sri Lanka won the World Cup in 1996, with new stars such as Ranatunga, Jayasuriya and Muralitharan playing the game as it had never been played before. The fact that Murali was a Tamil didn't go unnoticed, although he has wisely kept out of politics throughout his career, unlike Ranatunga and Jayasuriya, who have both become MPs.

It's easy for the British to be pious about this dreadful civil war, but we mustn't forget that we had problems on our own doorstep, in Northern Ireland, which also lasted for 30 years. There too sport — particularly rugby union which unites all Ireland — played a role in maintaining some form of unity during those dark years.

At the time we were heading to Sri Lanka, there was a hint of trouble in the air. Only Sri Lanka Airlines were flying into Colombo, the others having bottled it because of Tamil planes bombing the airbase next to the airport the day before we arrived. When it happened most Sri Lankans were watching their team lose to Australia in the final of the 2007 World Cup, so that meant two lots of bad news for the poor Sri Lankans to contend with.

To be honest, the bombing sounds a bit more dramatic than it really was. The local *Island* newspaper described the bombers as five Czech light planes which had been assembled from kits smuggled in by the Tamil rebels, and reported that between them they had dropped four small bombs. Still, to someone whose airport hassle is normally confined to lost luggage and late planes it was a rude awakening to the realities of life on the 'Jewel of the Indian Ocean'.

We'd been asked to travel down to Galle, on the southwestern tip of the island, one of the areas worst affected by the tsunami. The journey from Colombo to Galle is only a hundred miles or so but takes several hours because the road hasn't fully recovered from the ravages of the tsunami. All along the way are sad memorials to those who died, an awful counterpoint to the palm tree-fringed beaches and resorts that line the coastal road. Offshore, the famous stilt fishermen ply their trade as if nothing had happened, but many must have been lost to the tsunami. The railway follows the same route along the coast and provided one of the most vivid images of the devastation at the time, when packed carriages were swept away by the sea.

A great many charities are doing work across the island to try to improve Sri Lanka's future, but our remit was just to bring cricket and a bit of fun to young people affected by the tsunami, a lot of whom had been orphaned by it.

Our local contact was not what we'd expected. Carla Browne was a sculptress who had virtually abandoned her English home to spend most of her time in Galle where she was selflessly trying to build a school to replace the one washed away by the sea. Keen to get to know all the local movers and shakers, she'd met the Sri Lanka Cricket manager for the area, Mr Warnaweera, who was looking for help to get the local youngsters back into cricket. Now, I don't know much about sculpture, and Carla didn't know much about cricket, but 'Warney', as naturally we insisted on calling him, turned out to be the main man, and within an hour of arriving in Galle, after a journey of twenty hours, we were working with a group of the most enthusiastic young cricketers we'd ever met.

Warney had played for Sri Lanka, just after they got their Test status – appropriately enough he was indeed a spin bowler – and after retirement had become a coach and administrator. Like all cricket administrators he moaned a lot, mainly about head office (the usual gripe), but his main concern at the time was getting the Galle Test ground ready for England's visit at the end of the year. (They did manage to play at the ground the following December and England were pretty grim in all aspects of their game, having particular trouble with Malinga, the likes of whom they'd never seen before.)

While the old town of Galle itself had been saved from the tsunami by the magnificent Galle Fort, built by the Dutch in the 17th century, and was now a World Heritage site; the newer town, including the Test cricket ground next to the fort, had been largely swept away.

On the day of the tsunami, Harrow School were due to play a match at the ground against a local school and, a few minutes before the scheduled start, were practising in front of the pavilion. As the waters swept across the pitch, players and spectators were able to scramble on top of the pavilion to save themselves. Sadly one parent, who had gone back to the hotel to fetch something, was lost to the waters, but if the tsunami had struck four minutes later, many more would have died.

The Harrow parents vowed to help rebuild the ground and our visit coincided with the first use of the new indoor cricket school they had paid for. Having raised the money and built a new indoor school myself back in England, I know how hard it is to do. Their efforts have at least provided a lasting memorial to one of the saddest days in Sri Lanka's troubled recent past.

The indoor school was certainly needed as it rained torrentially for most of our stay in Galle. The kids would have willingly played outside whatever the weather, though, as Warney had put Sri Lanka Cricket scholarships up for grabs for the best three cricketers. Because the tsunami had devastated facilities everywhere in the area, he'd never seen any of the kids before, since they were from the less privileged schools. The talent on show was extraordinary.

For years Sri Lankan cricket has been dominated by the 'posh' schools, which are modelled on English public schools.

Warney in particular wanted to expand his pool of talent, if nothing else to show off to his bosses in Colombo. Galle hasn't produced too many Test players, but the one local hero was Lasith Malinga, he of the strange slinging delivery and mad hair. In England the coaches would soon have stopped him bowling like that, but cricketing eccentricity is encouraged in Sri Lanka, much to their credit. Despite his unusual action, he remains one of the most accurate and lethal bowlers of fast yorkers anywhere in the world today.

That evening we decamped to Carla's for dinner, which was a wonderfully boozy affair. Although we learnt a lot about each other over the evening, none of us could remember what it was in the morning.

After some days, the rain relented enough for us to play outdoors, just down the road at Koggala. A victim of my generation, I decided to take in the railway route because Galle station looked just like an old Great Western Railway country station, even down to the cream and chocolate brown colour scheme. Funny the things our empire left behind.

There was a reasonable cricket ground in Koggala, which lies inland and so had been protected from the tsunami. Surprisingly, though, it was surrounded by rugby pitches. Rugby's a big game in Sri Lanka, and is especially popular among the Muslim minority. We were told that this is because Muslims face a degree of discrimination in cricket, though this is denied by the authorities. Interestingly, the great Sri Lankan cricketer Dilshan changed one of his forenames from Mohammed to Tillekeratne to emphasise his Singhalese roots, so there may be something in this. In a similar vein, the Pakistani Test player Yousuf Youhana became

Mohammad Yousuf, showing that politics and religion are never far away in the subcontinent.

With the three scholarships at stake, the cricket at Koggala was fiercely competitive. At the end of the day we all had to go back to Carla's for more beer and whisky to discuss who should get the prizes. To be honest, I thought this process was a bit inappropriate, as most of these kids were just getting into the game and we were just there to encourage them and give them some fun. Still, 'proper' cricket is all about competitiveness, and Warney was in charge, so we went along with it.

Decisions made, the presentation ceremony the following day was a grand affair with a band, dancers and speeches, and everyone in school uniform. English was translated into Singhalese. Singhalese was translated into English. Everyone was thanked, no one was missed out. Interminable. All the kids wanted to know was who the lucky ones were. There was much whooping when the 'Koggala Three' were finally announced. Everyone also got a certificate for just having been there, which I know might sound too egalitarian, but most of these kids were making their first steps into sport so it was right to make them feel rewarded. Now they were on Warney's database, so hopefully not lost to the game.

The scholarships were in Colombo, so these few days had completely changed the lives of the Koggala Three, who were now on the fast track. Who knows, another Malinga might be on the way.

Only a few months later, England played at Galle, a game which coincided with a charity project opening that was much bigger than ours. At Seenigama, a village twenty kilometres north of Galle which had been devastated by the tsunami, the MCC had used proceeds from an International XI match at Lord's in 2005 to open a Centre of Excellence. This included not just a new cricket ground, the Seenigama Oval, but also educational and medical facilities for the whole area. Sri Lankan cricketers such as Murali, Kumar Sangakkara and Chaminda Vaas have been very involved in this project, to make sure that it thrives in the future. The cricketing fraternity worldwide has come together to help Sri Lanka recover from the effects of the tsunami.

The tsunami was a natural catastrophe. Now it was time to see if cricket could help heal the wounds of two manmade catastrophes: the 30-year Tamil civil war and the Lahore bombings of 3 March 2009, when the Sri Lankan Test team bus was attacked and the players had to be airlifted out. The Tamil civil war had left Sri Lanka traumatised, and the Lahore bombing, coming so soon after the England team had narrowly avoided attack in Mumbai, had left the ICC similarly affected.

Despite criticisms of the ICC, it is an organisation genuinely committed to nurturing the game in both existing cricket countries and 'new' ones. The Lahore bombings, which led to Pakistan losing all of its home games (and to exclusion from the riches of the IPL for that matter) threatened to overwhelm the ICC's plans to celebrate its 100th anniversary in 2009.

It decided to attack the problem head on, so to speak, and announced a programme called 'Catch the Spirit' at the

India/Pakistan warm-up game at The Oval in London, three months to the day since the Lahore bombings. This was to raise money to help the victims of the bombings, and to run cricket programmes aimed at helping the disadvantaged in the four subcontinental countries. Sri Lanka was chosen as the first of these. The sell-out crowd of 20,000 was generous, and with other donations over $100,000 was raised. Yes, the ICC deals in dollars; how the old members of the Imperial Cricket Conference would have harrumphed.

We must have done something right in Galle, because the charity was asked to see if we could use cricket to get ex-Tamil Tiger child soldiers reintegrated back into mainstream Sri Lankan society, following the ceasefire in early 2009. It is estimated that between January 2009 when the Tamil capital Kilinochchi fell, and May later that year, some 40,000 Sri Lankans died in the remaining Tamil strongholds in the north-east of the island. Truly, they were the killing fields of Kilinochchi. This was obviously very serious stuff, with governments, aid agencies and human rights organisations all involved, never mind the cricket authorities trying to do their best. We soon discovered that Sri Lankan cricket is not just about cricket, it's about politics, life and, sadly, death.

Michael Atherton has stated that 'even Zimbabwean cricket is less political than Sri Lanka's governing body' and I haven't heard anyone argue with him. There was certainly politics in the air in Colombo, where road blocks and armed troops were everywhere – a very different atmosphere from laid-back Galle.

But we had a good reminder of Galle, staying in the Galle Face Hotel, a wonderful relic from the days of empire, which overlooked both the Indian Ocean and Galle Face Green, where hundreds of young Sri Lankans were playing impromptu cricket. I read that in 1891 Tommy Kelaart took W.G. Grace's wicket on Galle Face Green. He got everywhere that W.G., didn't he?

More politics was evident as we were ushered into Nishantha Ranatunga's office, at the Sinhalese Sports Club ground in Colombo. Nishantha is the brother of Arjuna, the man who led Sri Lanka to its famous victory in the 1996 World Cup and as Hon. Sec. of Sri Lanka Cricket is very much the main man. With ICC approval and money behind us, we'd assumed that this was just a courtesy visit to explain what we were trying to achieve. My years in advertising should have taught me – never assume anything. Mr Ranatunga wasn't particularly impressed with the ICC – and us as their agents – parking their tanks on his lawn.

I've been protective myself in similar situations, so maybe it wasn't surpising, but his lack of enthusiasm made life difficult. After an hour or so of discussion, I thought it was time to beat a tactical retreat and see if a few cold Singha beers could come up with a solution. But as we were leaving the ground, Sri Lanka Cricket's marketing man, who'd been silent throughout the meeting, took me aside and said, 'Don't worry, we'll get it through, just be patient. There's already been some movement. The first schools cricket for over twenty years between Tamils from Jaffna and Singhalese from Colombo has just taken place, and this is an obvious next step.'

He could see the benefits of the proposed work: a great story of the national sporting body doing groundbreaking work with cricket, and the ICC paying for it. He suggested we see a woman called Manori, who'd gained access to these ex-child soldiers in camps in the north of the island and was using art to get them communicating again, with a lot of success. She was right that sport isn't the only way to get through to troubled kids, anything that stimulates in a positive way can work, but she also agreed that cricket seemed a perfect fit for Sri Lanka's cricket-crazy kids.

The other agencies all seemed keen. The British Council liked it. UK Sport liked it. The British High Commission liked it. The Ministry of Sports liked it. The Ministry of Justice liked it. All suggested that we should see UNICEF and the Bureau of the Commissioner General of Rehabilitation. UNICEF we knew about, but the bureau was a new one.

When we entered the office of the bureau it was with some trepidation, given our tricky meeting with Mr Ranatunga. Colonel Modestus Fernando, the deputy commissioner, welcomed us, though not with open arms. However, this was because he only had one arm; the other, he said, had been blown off in the Tamil war, so he shook hands with his brown prosthetic arm – normal for him, not at all a usual experience for us.

He was quite happy to talk about what had happened to him and what was happening now in the north of the island. He'd been a victim of the war, but was full of optimism for the future. An impressive fellow, and one who was very supportive of what we were trying to achieve – as he said, 'Reconciliation is the only answer.' He's obviously right. This is what's happening in South Africa now, post apartheid, and in our own Northern Ireland, and it's what's got to happen in Israel if there's ever going to be peace.

Colonel Fernando wanted us to go to visit one of the Tamil child soldier 'rehabilitation' camps in the country-side near Ambepussa, a town about 30 miles north-east of Colombo. I wanted to take the train to Ambepussa, from another 'Great Western Railway' station, Colombo Fort, not just for nostalgic reasons but because it looked safer. However, I was outvoted, so had to endure a typically mad, bad and dangerous Sri Lankan drive along a main road with potholes worse than Hertfordshire, which is saying something. From the speed at which we travelled I would imagine Jeremy Clarkson must be popular in Sri Lanka — I wanted to ask the driver if he was a fan of *Top Gear*, but I was too terrified to speak.

Ambepussa is a stop-off point on the way up to one of Sri Lanka's biggest tourist attractions, the Pinnewala Elephant Sanctuary. We dropped in, bought our obligatory carved elephants, had a couple of beers, and headed off a side road up to the rehabilitation centre. The countryside changed to sunken paddy fields with narrow roads between them, before giving way to dense and very green forests.

The rehab centre was not as we'd expected.

We were stopped by armed guards manning a check-point which marked its entrance. A high barbed-wire fence climbed up the hillside, and scattered on the open ground were wooden blockhouses. I'd read that the famous movie *Bridge over the River Kwai* had been shot in Sri Lanka, and this place could have doubled for the prison camp, except for one detail: all the inmates were children.

We were met by the camp commandant, who was a sur-prisingly jolly fellow, and was happy for us to ask whatever we wanted about the camp and the children. It turned out that he was a teacher, but his military uniform made it obvious that he was also in the army.

In any war there is wrong on both sides, but it seemed hard to justify such extreme conditions for the children. The LTTE (Liberation Tigers of Tamil Eelam), aka the Tamil Tigers, had insisted throughout the war that every Tamil family give up one of their children to their war effort. Most didn't end up fighting. Some worked in the kitchens, others carried messages, or became drivers or labourers – any of the dull but necessary jobs that need to be done when you're fighting a war. The LTTE had been well armed and apparently trained by the Libyans. They had been a formidable fighting force, one of the reasons that the war lasted so long.

We were told that in the chaos of war a lot of the children in the camp didn't know whether their parents had survived or not, and that they were being kept there while efforts were made to find their families. We weren't allowed to talk to the children about their individual circumstances, but the camp commandant said that sometimes the results of the searches were extraordinary. Some parents, assuming their children had died, had emigrated to Canada or the UK, so efforts then had to be made to reunite them. Meanwhile, the children attended lessons, mainly learning basic literacy, as many had never been to school before.

After hearing such stories, it seemed trite to ask if any of the children would like to play a bit of cricket. There was a stony area that had been cleared for a football pitch, but no one had tried cricket before.

'Why not?' the colonel said. 'I'll see if any want to play.' Soon a small group had assembled, one by one. They approached us with some trepidation, but reassured by the

boss that we were OK. We'd brought along the usual assort-
ment of plastic bats, wickets and tapeballs. The children were
curious. They'd seen cricket on TV, but they'd never played
it — and this in a country that's crackers about cricket.

So we just started with the basic stuff — batting, fielding,
catching and bowling. As always seems to be the case, a game
of sorts just happened, with no rules apart from having a
good time. Many of these children had never played anything, ever. The war had stolen their childhood from them,
and this was to be the start of the effort to give it back.

The bell went for lunch, and the children scampered off.
We went too, pleased that we'd demonstrated that by strip-
ping out the complexities of the game it was possible to
get the children playing almost immediately. If we could get
these children down to Colombo, then real progress could
be made.

However, we were quiet in the car back. In spite of the
positive reception we had received, we realised that we'd just
been to a children's prison camp, and it wasn't a nice feeling.

Back in Colombo we had a meeting with UNICEF who
were very involved with the child soldier issue. We hoped that
they'd be able to help us in our attempts to get approval for
the programme. UNICEF's country representative, Philippe
Duamelle, an anglophone and anglophile Frenchman, could
not have been more helpful. He'd heard about our plans
from all the other meetings we'd attended and from the
many emails that had been flying around. It's amazing how
the political 'bush telegraph' works in countries such as Sri
Lanka.

For a start, as an anglophile Frenchman (not that common) he knew about cricket and liked it. More importantly,

he understood the importance of cricket to Sri Lanka – how it had the power to unite the country, and how it might be able to unlock the lives of the child soldiers. He explained the magnitude of the problem. There were up to 45,000 'internally displaced' children under eighteen in Sri Lanka at the end of the war. Some people regarded them as just as guilty as adult soldiers, and so UNICEF had been running a poster campaign across the country, under the theme 'Bring Back the Child'. One of the posters featured a child in army uniform carrying a gun, the barrel of which metamorphosed into a cricket bat, along with the line 'He wants to be a cricketer not a child soldier'. It was a simple powerful message that, as an old adman, I'd have been proud to have been associated with back home in England.

Philippe said that UNICEF was very concerned about camps such as Ambepussa. There was another much bigger one at Vavuniya in the north of the island, closer to the Tamil heartland. Apart from the obvious problems of being separated from their families, most of the children were suffering from post-traumatic stress disorder, and the 'camp' environment was not a good place to help this condition.

As it was the end of another very long day, Philippe asked if we'd like to join him for supper at his favourite restaurant. A definite yes from us. We found ourselves in an unlikely place for a Frenchman to choose – the Cricket Club Café, 34 Queen's Road, a sports bar complete with an Aussie barmaid. As Harry Hill often says, 'What are the chances of that happening, eh?'

We discovered that Philippe had spent time at school in England. As I'd spent time at school in France, my francophilia matched his anglophilia, and a jolly time was had by all. But most importantly he promised to use his influence with the Sri Lankan government and the Sri Lankan cricket authorities to help get our project off the ground.

This he certainly did. UNICEF deal at the very top level of government. Now is not the time to go into all the difficult politics surrounding the end of the war, suffice to say that they were concerned about 'victorious' Sri Lankan military men being in charge of the rehabilitation process, and of the children being kept in secure camps.

The ICC also played their part in reassuring the Sri Lankan cricket authorities that we weren't a threat to them and that good could come out of the programme. This pincer movement removed all the obstacles, so by the time we returned to Sri Lanka only a few months later, the Ambepussa camp had been closed, and children from there and some from the Vavuniya camp had either been returned to their families or had been enrolled at the Ratmalana Hindu College.

I managed to avoid the mad 30-minute tuk-tuk drive from the centre of Colombo to Ratmalana by taking the train to Mount Lavinia, a wonderful colonial resort a world away from the issues we were encountering, and only a mad five-minute tuk-tuk drive to Ratmalana.

Ratmalana College was also a world away from the Ambepussa camp. It's a well-established Hindu school that respects the religion of its pupils and, apart from the brightly-coloured Hindu temple, was almost English public school-like, with a central courtyard surrounding cloisters, off which ranged the classrooms. The all-important playing fields were nearby, and marquees had been erected for a whole array of bigwigs who'd turned up to see what was going on.

The children were wearing smart school uniforms, a big

change from the green stripes of the Tamil Tiger militia they'd been wearing previously. The plan was a simple one: to work with about 50 or so of the 273 Tamil pupils to find 24 of them to train up as 'peer leaders'. These could then go back to their communities to help other young people get attuned to life in the mainstream. 'Peer leaders' is one of those charity industry buzz-words that has replaced old-fashioned concepts such as 'good egg'. In this instance, it meant finding someone who could communicate well and who was sympathetic to the problems and worries of their mates.

There were some quizzical looks on the faces of the on-looking guests as the plan was unveiled. The boss of the reha-bilitation commission, Brigadier Sudantha Ranasinghe was among the puzzled, but in true military style he was happy to give it a go. He actually rather frightened me; a huge man with a fine moustache, wearing his medal-bedecked uni-form with pride. We talked a lot. The war had been so long that it had taken up most of his army career, and he was very pleased that it was over. He also seemed genuinely keen not to be seen as the victor, believing that it was more important for Sri Lanka to put this sad past behind it and go forward positively.

He explained, in the nicest possible way, that the Tamil problem was a product of British colonialism, because they were favoured by the imperial Brits and pretty much ran the civil service, even though they were very much the minority 'newcomers'. Independence changed all that, and the rest, as they say, is history.

Getting the children to play was difficult. Not because they didn't like the game, but because the whole concept

of 'play' was still alien to them. They'd all come out of regu-
lated, dangerous situations, so just to have some fun somehow
seemed wrong. After a while though, and greatly helped by
the local coaches — some of whom, like Upul Chandana, had
played Test cricket — the message got through that they were
safe, that everyone there wanted to help them, and that they
might be chosen as very special young people to go back to
their communities to spread the word.

In a way lunchtimes were the best part of our days in
Sri Lanka. They were a time when all could relax a bit and
chew over, so to speak, what they'd done in the morning.
The children would talk not just about cricket, but about life
in general and what the future might hold for them. They
talked about going to university, becoming teachers, lawyers
and accountants. Some had realised they were good at the
game and wanted to become famous Sri Lankan cricketers.
Some still bore the marks of war, like Sailan — probably about
12 years old — whose arms were both badly scarred. But the
key thing was that they weren't talking about the war; they
were becoming children again.

Lunch was the same every day: vegetable curry, rice,
purri and a very sweet pudding. Wonderful. I wish more
Indian restaurants in England would produce food like
this. Simple, cheap and natural, without the need for lurid
chicken tikka masala or stomach-churningly hot vindaloos.
All the locals thought it was hysterical that we loved the
food, but of course they hadn't been to Brick Lane in
London, the Curry Triangle in Birmingham or Belgrave
Gate, Leicester.

The cricket was a mixture of whatever suited. The older
children wanted the hard ball game, to bowl like Malinga

rather than Murali, and to smash the ball like Dilshan. The girls preferred tapeball, and enjoyed making up their own tapeballs in their favourite colours.

After a day or two, the leaders were becoming evident. They were the ones who wanted to be captain, who were happy getting the fielders organised, and, to be honest, the ones who were the most natural sportsmen and women. This isn't to denigrate those who just tried their best (I was one of those who did his best as a young cricketer but never really succeeded, and I'm no better now), but for the purposes of this programme a degree of leadership along with some sporting ability was the best combination.

All the front-runners were discussed with the coaches and teachers, who knew their individual circumstances. Some would not be able to leave for a while, until good homes had been found for them. Others were ready to go to safe new homes, with the war now a more distant memory.

Apparently the process of rehabilitation in Sri Lanka is controversial, and I've mentioned the concerns of UNICEF. However, two of the chosen leaders had been in the thick of the action. Gopi had been a driver for the Tamil Tigers, and Mathi's job had been clearing up bodies from the streets. Both were now ready to re-enter society, with a new and more positive view of life, and the wonderful and extraordinary thing was that cricket had played a part in that process.

Graduation day at the Singhalese Sports Club in Colombo was when it all came together, and this was where the Sri Lanka Cricket Board proved that it was big enough to change its mind.

The club has a wonderful ground. The Lord's of Sri Lanka

might be over-egging it a bit, but it's an impressive sight, with a massive old-fashioned scoreboard at one end — so much nicer than those horrid digital ones. Call me old fashioned but give me big white numbers painted on black metal squares any day. Actually, the scoreboard has to be really big, to handle those long Sri Lankan names. Goodness knows what a Sri Lankan Scrabble board looks like.

UNICEF had dressed the stadium with banners and flags, the media were massed, the presentation platform was in place and there was even a crowd. Hundreds of schoolchildren were there to watch the demonstration games going on across the ground. It looked like a Test match was about to start, but in a way it was more important. It was the start of the long road back to normality for these children of the war.

Everyone made a speech, as is always the way. All the partners had their say — the British High Commission, the British Council, the Sri Lankan government, my friend the brigadier and UNICEF. The Sri Lankan Cricket Board's Mr Ranatunga was fulsome in his praise too, which was good to hear and, frankly, it was good of him to be seen to have changed his view.

But the most important speeches were by the children themselves. Sailan, his scars almost hidden by his smart blue and white Sri Lanka cricket shirt, summed up what they felt about the week. 'Cricket has shown me that my glass is half full, that I should look to my future, and not at the bad things in my past.' I'm afraid he'd learnt the 'glass half full' phrase from us, and he deliberately included it in his speech as a joke — a nice touch that showed us what a great little leader he'll become.

The good news is that the MCC has stayed involved in Sri Lanka by supporting a new cricket ground south of Jaffna at Mankulam, in the Tamil heartland, on land which was given to Murali. This work was celebrated at a dinner at Lord's during the Sri Lankan tour in 2011. Also at Lord's, in the 2011 Sir Colin Cowdrey 'Spirit of Cricket' lecture, the great Sri Lankan cricketer Kumar Sangakkara first bravely castigated the Sri Lankan government's overweening influence on the game, then, after a spellbinding 90-minute talk, finished with this positive message: 'I am Tamil, Singhalese, Muslim, a Burgher. I am Buddhist, a Hindu, a follower of Islam and Christianity. I am today, and always, proudly Sri Lankan.'

Perhaps the best way to finish on Sri Lanka is to quote Arthur C. Clarke, who wrote *2001 – A Space Odyssey*, and who spent much of his life in Sri Lanka: 'And always it is the same, the slender palm trees leaning over the white sand, the warm sun sparkling on the waves as they break on the inshore reef. This alone is real; the rest is but a dream from which I shall presently awake.' Sri Lanka is indeed a beautiful place, which is home to many different peoples. It deserves its peace and its place at the top of cricket's table.

Each of the regions featured so far – the UK, the Caribbean, the Americas, the Middle East and the Indian subcontinent – have their individual issues where cricket can be of help, from giving disabled people the chance to enjoy sport again to breaking down barriers between ethnic groups. Part two of the book concerns countries in sub-Saharan Africa where there are different common issues, such as poverty and the legacy of the colonial era, but where again cricket can play a role in helping to improve the lives of those affected.

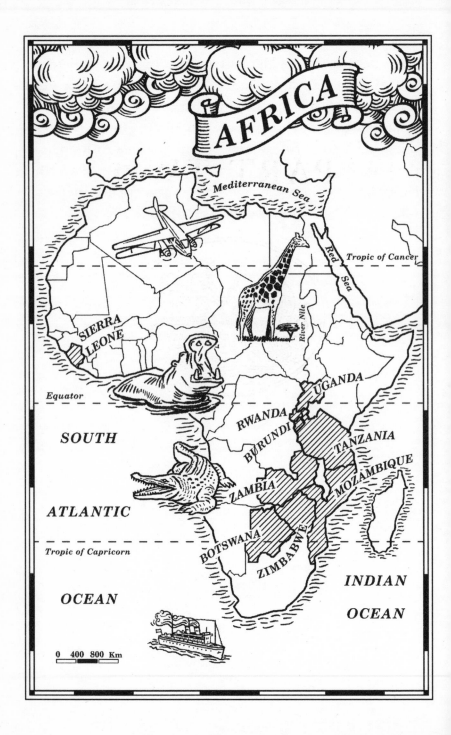

PART TWO

9

INTO AFRICA – LIVINGSTONE, ZAMBIA, I PRESUME?

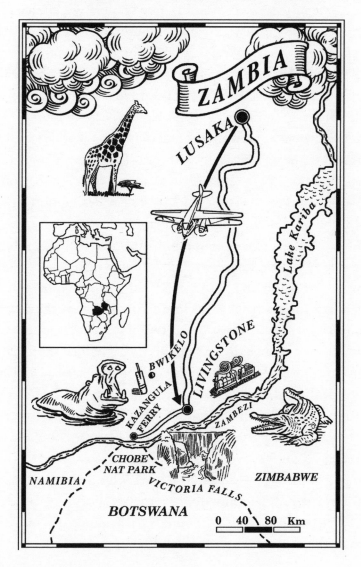

WE HAD BEEN ACHIEVING good results using cricket in various countries we'd worked in. It was those efforts that got us invited by the British government to form part of their multi-faceted delegation to a UN conference in Africa. We hadn't yet done any work there, but just from reading the newspapers we knew there would be many challenges to overcome, and that it would be interesting to see how cricket could help.

Zambian Airways' strap line is 'Changing The Way Africa Flies', which wasn't really what I wanted to hear as our flight to Livingstone from Lusaka banked steeply over Victoria Falls, so close that you could almost feel the spray on your face. The original name of the Falls, Mosi-oa-Tunya or 'The Smoke that Thunders', is a much better name than Livingstone's more sycophantic version – it's a perfect description of the astonishing sight and sound of them.

Many famous places disappoint on first sight. Stonehenge doesn't look that impressive as you speed (or more likely crawl) past it on the A303. And although Wimbledon's a fine place to watch the Brits lose tennis matches, the Centre Court's a bit small, because, well, tennis courts are quite small. But Mosi-oa-Tunya doesn't disappoint, whether approached from near or far. Livingstone discovered the falls in 1855 and rapturously said that: 'Scenes so lovely must have been gazed upon by angels in their flight.' One hundred and fifty years later the scenes gazed upon by the passengers of Zambian Airways Flight 500 were just as lovely.

Zambia used to be called Northern Rhodesia, imperiously and hubristically so named when the territory was annexed by Cecil Rhodes' British South Africa Company in 1895, one of the British Empire's less edifying periods.

The town of Livingstone itself was founded 32 years after the famous explorer's death, in 1905. This was just in time for it to welcome the by-then late Cecil Rhodes' famous Cape to Cairo railway as it crossed the Zambezi River on a precarious-looking bridge made in Darlington. The railway never made it all the way to Cairo – it runs from Cape to Congo as it happens – but this must be its highlight.

Livingstone now is one of those old colonial towns that haven't changed much since they were founded: low buildings line a long main street, Wild West-style. The main street is called Mosi-oa-Tunya Road, and leads all the way to the great falls and the border with Zimbabwe, which was the southern half of Rhodes' old Rhodesia. It was the venue for a United Nations conference on sport that we had been invited to, which would eventually lead to our getting involved with work in five African countries: Zimbabwe, Uganda, Rwanda, Tanzania and Sierra Leone, though the reason we had been invited would not be explained to us until later.

The conference was part of a sort of nine-Test series of conferences, from Australia to Zambia, set up at no doubt vast cost to celebrate and pontificate on the UN's 'International Year of Sport and Physical Education'.

Now I'm used to conferences, normally sales conferences where new advertising is presented to hard-bitten sales people who aren't the slightest bit interested in it. That is always the hard part, but by definition someone else is paying, there's normally not much work to be done after the advertising has been presented to the comatose, and the venue is generally nice. I remember a particularly good one in the Bahamas for Toyota where we didn't even have to show the ads, and where our wives could come too, which was very jolly, and improved my tennis no end.

The Fairmount Hotel and Casino, Mosi-oa-Tunya Road, Livingstone was indeed a very nice place, with a lovely pool and outdoor bar and restaurant, shaded by a magnificent jacaranda tree. This all fitted in with my advertising experience of conferences, but everything else was very different. For a start we had to pay for everything, including getting there, which was something of a shock. Secondly, we had something to do – the brief from our friends at the Foreign Office, from the Department of Culture, Media and Sport and from UK Sport was to meet and greet as many of the delegates as possible. These came from all over sub-Saharan Africa. We were to tell them about our work and buy them drinks if they wanted any. At its most trite, this was just showing off and drinking, both of which I have to admit that I enjoy and do quite well, but the results of this 'work' were very different to what I'd expected.

We were welcomed by the president of Zambia, Mr Levy Mwanawasa, a massive, smiling man with a handshake even more bone-crunching than Mike Gatting's. He read out a message from the UN Secretary General, Kofi Annan, praising the benefits of sport in some rather fine sentences, 'Sport is a universal language. At its best it can bring people together, no matter what their origin, background, religious beliefs or economic status. And when young people participate in sports or have access to physical education, they can experience real exhilaration, even as they learn the ideals of teamwork and tolerance.'

The joint sponsors of the conference were the various British government agencies already mentioned. President

Mwanawasa's opening speech was responded to by the Right Hon. Tessa Jowell, Secretary of State at the Department for Culture Media and Sport. It struck me at the time that the quantity of British participation seemed to be over-egging it a bit — after all this was just a conference in 'a small town in Africa, just a small town in Africa', as the football chant goes. Still, I wasn't going to complain as we were ushered to the Jacaranda Bar for welcoming drinks.

It turned out that one of the reasons for the Brits' interest was that Mwanawasa was one of a pretty small group of African leaders who wasn't corrupt and who was keen on democracy — his predecessor, President Chiluba, had been on trial the previous year for stealing £23 million in state funds. Mwanawasa was also one of the few African leaders to condemn Mugabe for turning neighbouring Zimbabwe into a 'sinking Titanic' as he daringly described it. Because of Zambia's relative stability, it was gaining at Zimbabwe's expense as dispossessed white farmers from Zimbabwe were encouraged to come there to help develop the country. So, he was a sensible man as well as a brave one. Sadly he died relatively young in 2008.

The conference speeches were mainly from earnest charity workers and academics from Europe and North America, lecturing everyone on why Africa was in such a terrible state. I felt a bit sorry for the African delegates, who it somehow seemed were being blamed for the situation. It was dispiriting to hear that all agreed that the aid policies of the West towards Africa for the past 50 years had entirely failed, despite hundreds of millions having been spent. A very bright Zambian economist called Dambisa Moyo has even written a book about this failure called *Dead Aid*.

The answers seemed so simple. 'What's needed are fair trade, education and good governance,' said a Swedish professor. 'Aid is one-way. Partnership is two-way,' added a Canadian economist, stating the bleeding obvious. 'We must progress from dependence to independence to interdependence,' proclaimed a South African expert, sounding like he had read it in a book. 'And if we want a long life we must have small families, rather than a short life in a large family,' which is neat.

All fine words, but the facts remain that Africa is the fastest urbanising continent in the world, that it has now joined India and China with a population of over a billion, and that, as the UN says, it is a continent of 'oceans of poverty containing small islands of wealth'.

Even the most committed observer can take only so much repetition of the same basic principles, and I managed to slip out in the afternoon to take in a bit of sun by the pool. A lot of other delegates had had the same idea, so I rushed for the only free sun lounger, managing, by reversing the usual cliché , to beat a German charity worker to it. Settling in to read *Heart of Darkness*, Joseph Conrad's equally dispiriting novel about Africa, I suddenly realised to my dismay that there on the next lounger was sat the Rt. Hon. Tessa Jowell MP, resplendent in a flowery summer frock, and half hidden behind her massive white handbag.

It reminded me of a very funny TV commercial for the *Economist* where a young businessman rushes onto a plane and the only spare seat is next to Dr Henry Kissinger, thus precluding any normal conversation about girls, the weather and football. Our hero is saved by his copy of the *Economist*, which suitably impresses Dr Kissinger.

I did at least have my copy of *Heart of Darkness* as my intellectual prop but still, it was plain that the Rt. Hon. lady didn't want to talk about Africa, but then to be honest neither did I. It's easy to forget that people in the limelight are still ordinary human beings, and that in this case she'd come to sit by the pool for exactly the same reason as me, so we talked platitudes and just enjoyed the sunshine.

I had a similar experience at Grace Road, Leicester, when the Rt. Hon. Kenneth Clarke MP sat down next to me one Saturday morning in the members' seats in front of the pavilion at a Leicestershire v Nottinghamshire championship match. He was Chancellor of the Exchequer at the time, but instead of discussing the public sector borrowing requirement, we drank a couple of pints of Everards and discussed the state of first-class cricket in England, a much more interesting and, dare I say it, more important subject.

It must run in the family, because funnily enough my father had a similar meeting with another Chancellor of the Exchequer, Nigel Lawson. Lawson was a local MP and was speaking at a public meeting in Leicester. There were very few people there, and at the end of his talk there was only one question from the floor, from my father, who asked if the chancellor could give him a lift home, since the buses were very unreliable, and the family home was on his way back to the M1. The chancellor, having consulted his advisors, agreed, and ended up having a cup of tea and scoffing biscuits, along with his advisors, at 21 Monsell Drive,

Aylestone, Leicester, which got all the neighbours' curtains twitching.

The conference was keen for delegates to see a bit of 'real' Africa, and organised for us all to visit the village of Bwikelo a few miles outside Livingstone. The contrast was astonishing, in that the village didn't look much different from how it would have been in Livingstone's day – just a group of mud huts with one bigger hut, which was the school.

As ever in Africa, the welcome was genuine, with all the school kids immaculately turned out in rows to greet us. Most of the sports charities at the conference were football-related, so a whole range of football activities took place. Naturally the kids loved this, as they were all fans of Man U, Chelsea, Liverpool and so on. Strangely, there were no fans of either of my two teams, Leicester City and Watford. Not to be outdone, we'd taken some Kwik Cricket plastic kits to demonstrate our game, so soon the kids were enjoying cricket too, to the astonishment of the non cricket-loving Danish, Dutch, Norwegian and German delegates.

Zambia does have some cricketing heritage. In the old colonial days, as part of Rhodesia, it took part in the Currie Cup competition with all the South African states, and Lusaka was the birthplace of Philippe Henri Edmonds, of Middlesex and England. But cricket was completely new to these young kids. That evening in the Jacaranda Bar we didn't have to impose ourselves on the African delegates, on the contrary, they all wanted to talk about cricket and how it could help them with their most disadvantaged kids, the disabled, for whom football is very difficult. Widespread poverty is the root cause of most of the disability in Africa, through bad diet and endemic diseases such as malaria.

Our simple demonstration had fired the imaginations of the local delegates. Rish Urio from the National Sports Complex in Dar es Salaam wanted us to come to Tanzania. Jasper Aligawesi said, 'No, come to Kampala in Uganda first.' But the most insistent were Ezra 'Ziggie' Zigarwe and Norman Nyaude from Zimbabwe. They'd driven up from Harare, begging and borrowing petrol along the way. He argued that their need was the greatest because Zimbabwe was suffering so much.

In the scrum of the Jacaranda Bar it was hard to have proper conversations, so we asked the locals if there was another bar in town. They said they'd take us all to the Rave Stone Nite Club, so long as we bought them a beer. The deal was struck, and after marching down Mosi-oa-Tunya Road we were soon ensconced as 'locals' in the Rave Stone, a wonderful open-air bar blaring out Congolese music until dawn. In fact, it still wasn't possible to have proper conversations, but because none of our new friends had any cash, we paid for all the beer and thus made friends for life. Simple.

The following day we were allowed a day off. Fresh air was needed, so Taonga Safaris took us over the Zambezi by the Kazungula ferry and into Botswana to see some hippos and crocs at the Chobe River Reserve. The Zambian customs guy manning the border wanted money to let us through, but as soon as I told him that I was a personal friend of President Levy Mwanawasa – indeed so much so that my hand was still hurting from his handshake – he waved us through. Corruption is endemic throughout much of Africa, and although Zambia has less than most countries it's hard to see how any real progress can be made in the continent until it is stopped.

A slightly bizarre tourist visit was made on the way back from Kazungula – I just had to take in the Livingstone Railway Museum. I'm such a child of the fifties that I'd found out about it from our new local friends, one of whom had worked for the Zambesi Sawmills Railway, which had left its engines at the museum when the railway was abandoned. E.D. Hamer's well-known bestseller (well, maybe not ...) *Steam Locomotives of Rhodesia Railways* describes it as 'this curious Mecca for enthusiasts of ancient African engines'. It certainly was; a museum of broken dreams and a forgotten past. Sad but wonderful.

Leaving Livingstone was also sad – the end of my first trip to the heart of Africa, with many new friends made along the way. Livingstone airport is one of those tiny airfields where you walk out to your plane rather than it coming to you, and with the obligatory tatty DC3 parked on the perimeter. In the departure lounge (only a bit bigger than my lounge at home) we bumped into a lot of our new friends. One was looking particularly agitated, however.

It was Nicholas Muramagi from the National Council of Sports in Uganda. He was waiting for his flight back to Kampala, but was remonstrating at the check-in desk. I asked him what the problem was, and his face dropped as he explained that he'd forgotten that you have to pay a five-dollar departure tax and that he didn't have any money. I know this sounds strange, but very few of the African delegates had any cash, as even educated 'middle class' civil servants are still, by our standards, very poor.

I said five dollars wasn't a problem and we sat down and chatted about the conference. He was a much quieter, more thoughtful man than most of the delegates. He hadn't joined us at the Rave Stone Nite Club, so we hadn't had much of a chance to talk, but he'd heard all about us from Jasper Aligawesi, and was extremely keen for us to come to Uganda. He'd had the idea of setting up a network of disability cricket across East Africa, starting in Uganda but hopefully then spreading out to Rwanda, Burundi, Tanzania and Kenya.

This was an extraordinary suggestion, especially as it was made just as our flight to Lusaka was being called, but Nicholas had a very determined look on his face, and a handshake as firm as President Mwanawasa's, so I thought, 'We mustn't let him down.' He also said that if we came back he'd pay me back the five dollars he owed me, another powerful incentive.

Less than a month later, three momentous days changed our lives, and indeed those of the entire country. On 6 July 2005, the UK, against all odds, was awarded the 2012 Olympics. This, I later discovered, was the real reason why we'd been invited to the sports conference in Livingstone in the first place. We were told that while the bigwigs including the Mayor of London (another Livingstone), Prime Minister

Blair and Lord Coe, had been doing some frantic last-minute networking in Singapore, our much softer approach (mainly involving buying a few rounds of Rhino lagers in the Rave Stone Nite Club) had also contributed to winning the cause. Again we'd been used by the Foreign Office, but in a very enjoyable way, so I didn't mind.

Then on 7 July, suicide bombers attacked buses and tubes in London, causing great loss of life, jolting us out of our false sense of security, and immediately ending the joy of the previous day.

Finally, on 8 July, the leaders of the G8 met in Gleneagles. They decided that the quickest way to help the poor countries of Africa was to cancel a large proportion of their debt. This initiative was led by Britain, possibly shamed by the state of a large part of its old empire. The overall mood that it was right and good for the developed world to help the developing world, made the potential of our making a small contribution to life in Africa even more relevant.

10

ZIMBABWE – FROM THE BREAD BASKET OF CENTRAL AFRICA TO A BASKET CASE

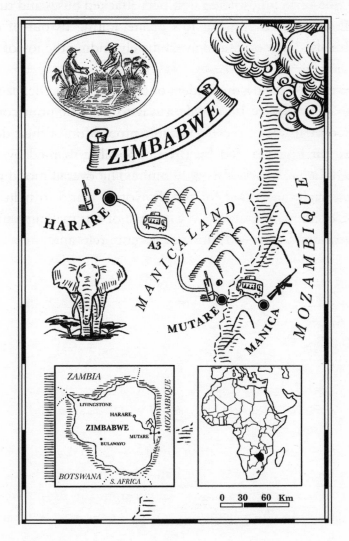

STELIOS KYRIAKIDES, with the grand title of Assistant Desk Officer, Zimbabwe Section, African Department (Southern) at the Foreign Office, said it was perfectly safe to travel to Zimbabwe to work, so long as you didn't talk politics, criticise the government or engage in illegal money changing. He also said that as it's effectively a police state we would be followed everywhere by informers hoping to catch us out transgressing in any of those ways.

But the England and Wales Cricket Board (ECB), thinking that we were somehow passing ourselves off as an official cricketing delegation, didn't agree that it was alright for us to go. We were bombarded by emails from various officials pleading with us to cancel our trip. The previous year, 2004, the England team had been forced by the ICC to tour Zimbabwe. They did so very reluctantly because of safety concerns. The ECB were actively trying to get Zimbabwe banned from international cricket, and Zimbabwe themselves were considering withdrawing from Test cricket because most of their good players – such as Andy Flower and Henry Olonga – had sought pastures new since their brave protest against Mugabe's government at the 2002 World Cup.

Mugabe always portrays himself as a great cricket lover, saying that he appreciates its 'civilising' capability. His splendid official residence is just over the road from the Harare Sports Club, but apparently he's rarely seen there lounging in a deckchair reading the paper, which is what I'd do if I lived there.

To be honest, I was with the ECB on this one as only a few months previously Mugabe had completed his 'Operation Murambatsvina', which charmingly translates as 'Drive out the Trash'. In this operation, homes in the squatter camps on the outskirts of Harare were bulldozed, leaving some 700,000 people homeless. The 'trash' referred to were mainly supporters of Morgan Tsvangarai's opposition MDC party. These appalling actions further weakened Mugabe's discredited democracy in the eyes of the world, but strengthened his position at home.

But then I remembered the promise we'd made to Norman Nyaude in Livingstone, and the fact that within days of meeting him he'd sent us an official invitation to help his newly formed Easterns Blind Cricket Club, based in Mutare, on the eastern edge of Zimbabwe. The letterhead of the club alone was almost enough persuasion – a cool-looking nyala antelope wearing shades and carrying a bat over its shoulder below the proud initials, E.B.C.C.

Norman's father Cyril met us at Harare airport in a scruffy white minibus with a strange smell inside. Because of the fuel shortage, Zimbabwe having run out of foreign currency to pay for imports, there were very few cars or buses about, so we were pleased to have any transport at all. Cyril had just made it to the airport before running out of fuel, so we stopped at the first petrol station, which had a queue of several hundred assorted vehicles waiting patiently in line.

Cyril asked if we had any US dollars, which we had, so we went straight to the head of the queue, filled up, and paid with our dollars. This rampant queue-jumping happened everywhere. US dollars bought you preference, while the poor locals with only Zimbabwe dollars, which were suffering inflation almost as high as Weimar Germany's in the 1920s, got nothing.

The road out east to Mutare from Harare is called the A3. One of the main roads out of London is also the A3 and also leads to many sporting facilities. There are some other similarities. Signs off the A3 in Zimbabwe point to places like Bromley, Wilton, Melfort and Theydon, which might be off our own A3, but these alternated with others such as Macheke, Umfeseri, Rasape and Nyazura, confirming that we were now in a very different land.

High-rise Harare soon became squatterland and then mile after mile of derelict farmland, land which once justified Zimbabwe/Rhodesia's reputation as the 'Bread Basket of Africa', but which now produced virtually nothing. Most of the (mainly white) farmers had had their land confiscated since 2000 and given to 'war veterans', who were in fact generally neither war veterans nor farmers, hence the dereliction.

Lots of good books have been written about the plight of these illegally dispossessed white Zimbabweans, such as Peter Godwin's *When a Crocodile Eats the Sun* and Andrew Meldrum's *Where We Have Hope*. It must never be forgotten that most of the victims of the Mugabe regime have been black. Nevertheless, it's estimated that of the 300,000 whites in Rhodesia in 1980, only about 20,000 are left in Zimbabwe, and most of them are either too old or too stubborn to leave.

It's a five-hour drive east to Mutare, so fittingly we stopped at the Halfway House as beers were needed. It was an African Dutch-style oasis of restaurant, antique shop, craft market and bar. It was doing hardly any business, so the vast car park was as empty as its 'zoo', which harboured an elderly lion and an even older cheetah.

Mikey had been in an emotional mood since we landed, as it was his first time in Africa or 'home' as he kept calling it. 'Home' really was Hackney, but I guess if your forefathers were shipped across the Atlantic from somewhere in Africa a couple of hundred years ago then you're entitled to call Africa 'home'. To liven him up a bit, we thought we'd use the empty car park to have an impromptu game of cricket, which went so well (Rodwell T, 3-0-27-2) that all the bored staff at the Halfway House either joined in playing or watched excitedly. You got the feeling that this was the first fun they'd had for a while.

Later, back on the A3, the strange smell in the minibus started to get even more powerful as the sun got hotter. I asked Cyril, who by now was my pal – we were both about the same age, and you don't see many old people in Africa – what the smell was. 'Probably from the morgue,' he said. 'To make a few more dollars we use the bus as a hearse every night, and last night was very busy.' A fair answer to a fair question, and it seemed rude to pry any further. Death is never far away in Africa – local AIDS rates of 40 per cent take away many people long before old age, so Cyril was unusual in being past 60. I didn't dare ask him what he felt like carrying dead bodies around every night, almost all of whom were younger than him.

The approach down to Mutare from Christmas Pass justifies its old description as 'the most picturesque city in Zimbabwe' and 'the gateway to the Eastern Highlands'. In its colonial guise as Umtali, it was a favourite place for holidays, being close to the Nyanga and Bvumba mountains, and its cooler climate made it a popular place for retirement. The founder of Rhodesia, Cecil Rhodes, had a fine home up in the mountains, which is now known as the Rhodes Nyanga Hotel.

Mutare was still a good place. The Main Street had become Herbert Chitepo Street, and featured a Wimpy Bar and a Nando's to keep Mikey stuffed with burgers and chicken, while our Holiday Inn on the corner of Aerodrome Road and Third Street was a jolly place. It's bar was full of the Zimbabwe football team enjoying themselves before playing an African Nations Cup match in Mutare the following night. I'm sure they thought we were English football agents, because they all wanted to talk. Most were based in South Africa, none wanted to come back to Zimbabwe and all wanted to play in England.

A few Zimbabweans have made it into English football. Bruce Grobbelaar's hard to forget, but there was also Peter Ndlovu and now Benjani Mwarawari. Only a month after we met the Zimbabwe team, some of them got their wish to play in England, as an exhibition match was played in Bradford between two rival Zimbabwean teams, Caps United and Highlanders FC. They obviously enjoyed themselves because after the match six of them disappeared into thin Yorkshire air and didn't return home!

Another man in the bar at the Holiday Inn was the local opposition MDC MP, who also wanted to talk. I told him about our briefing from the Foreign Office and he understood, but he reiterated that Mugabe's spies were everywhere. 'One of them will be in this bar,' he said, and I suddenly thought it might be him, but I've lived to tell the tale, so it obviously wasn't.

We were all excited at the prospect of seeing Norman again and helping to coach the members of the Easterns Blind Cricket Club. Cyril arrived in the morning, fresh (if that's the right word) from the morgue, to take us to the Mutare Sports Club. It was next to the Beira-Mutare-Harare railway line, but still in a beautiful spot close to the centre of town. In the old days, it had been the sporting and social centre for Umtali's whites, and the cricket pitch was still there in good order, although the nets were a bit threadbare. The pavilion was imposing if scruffy, but to be honest a lot of cricket pavilions are like that in England. There's never enough money to keep everything shipshape.

Norman had been up to the local blind school to fetch the kids. There were about a dozen of them, a mix of girls and boys, ranging from only six or seven years old to teenagers. Apart from one white boy, all were black, and their eyesight varied between very bad and total blindness. One or two of the 'black' children were albinos, who came into the former category – harsh sunlight is a real problem for albinos and leads, sadly, to poor eyesight.

We'd brought Geoff with us, who for years was wicketkeeper in the England Blind Cricket team. For obvious reasons, in blind cricket the keeper is 'allowed' some sight, but Geoff, now a middle-aged man, probably had only about 25 per cent vision, and it was deteriorating. He'd taught blind children at school in England, so this, combined with his sporting prowess, made him the ideal person to introduce the game to the kids. We also had Mikey, who'd been Geoff's coach in the England team, and who even the completely blind kids could tell was black, and therefore 'one of them'.

Geoff started the day with a talk about what blind cricket had done for him. He'd come to it late, he said, and wished he'd started as young as most of his audience, because then, he said, he'd have been so much better. Through cricket he'd made new friends, achieved excellence and been able to travel overseas, playing the game in India and Australia.

After all this inspiration, the kids couldn't wait to get started and Mikey took over, explaining the game bit by bit by involving each and every kid individually. He soon got them playing. A lot of the game is about confidence, and about knowing that you're not going to get hurt. The wide-open spaces of a cricket pitch make this the perfect place for blind kids to gain that confidence.

A couple of hours in the hot sun were enough. The kids were not used to getting much exercise, so soon got tired, and the break for lunch at midday was well timed. A huge tub of mealie – the local staple made from maize – was brought in. It fills you up but doesn't have much goodness in it, although that didn't seem to matter to the kids, who scoffed it down, obviously starving hungry. There was some indeterminate meat in there as well which, while dodgy to our spoilt taste buds, was again devoured in minutes.

Mikey sat on the ground with the kids in the shade of a giant baobab tree, next to the scoreboard. I was some yards away, chatting to one of the groundsmen, Fradrick, but could see that his presence alone was transfixing them. They talked a bit, but most of the time they simply sat in silence, happy in each other's company.

I often feel that we talk too much – we have a need to fill space with meaningless words. The effect of Mikey's mere presence on the kids emphasised the power of silence. The street word is chillin', but it's just silence, pure and simple. Simon and Garfunkel sang about it in the 'Sound of Silence'. The lyrics of that song seem to describe Mikey's powerful presence amongst those children, and indeed aspects of blindness too – the darkness, the fear and the need for help.

I've since been on trendy business away days where the facilitator drones on inexorably about the power of silence. But there is truth in this. Try it. Just sit there and don't say anything, even in company. It's very therapeutic.

After lunch, Geoff talked to the kids about how much blind cricket is played around the world, and said that if they were really good they too could play for their country. They were keen anyway, and had obviously enjoyed their first morning's cricket, but this revelation only increased their interest. Perhaps in the back of the minds of the older ones was the thought of getting out of Zimbabwe and staying out, like those errant footballers.

Zimbabwe's cricket is regional, and Mutare is the centre of the Manicaland region, whose coaches had come along to watch, because they wanted to know how to teach blind cricket. Afterwards, we went out with them for a few cold Zambezi lagers at the Bulldog Bar on the main street. Despite Zimbabwe's problems, they were genuinely trying to get better at cricket and, all local black guys themselves, were enthusiastic partners in the Zimbabwe Cricket Union's efforts to 'indigenise' the game, which has to be the answer, since most of the whites have left.

Rhodesia/Zimbabwe had regularly produced great cricketers, such as Colin Bland and Graeme Hick, as well as others less famous, such as Brian Davison and the late Paddy Clift, who I remember watching at Grace Road, Leicester, in the

1970s. However, change had been forced on the game and these Zimbabwean coaches were embracing it. The ZCU's motto is 'Excellence through Diversity' and these coaches were certainly doing their best to achieve that, in circumstances that could not be more difficult – little food, no petrol and ludicrous inflation.

In these appalling circumstances, it seemed petty that the ECB and the ICC were trying to exclude Zimbabwe from international cricket. They were doing their best, they were proper cricket people, and I was ashamed that we were the only overseas people trying to help. I thought that surely South Africa, just down the road, and much wealthier than Zimbabwe, should be helping. But when I asked it seemed that this was tiptoeing into politics, and the coaches didn't reply. They were silent.

We'd brought some spare kit with us, which they were so happy to have that they insisted on us taking it straight away to their office, which was along the road next to Mutare Hospital. We carried on chatting; no silence now – it's amazing what cricket people find to talk about. Idly looking out of the window, I saw Cyril's minibus bus/hearse arriving at the hospital, and leaving a few minutes later with its axles a bit closer to the ground. More business for the morgue – just another normal, sad day in Mutare.

Over the next few days, the kids we were working with gained such confidence with bat and ball that they started shouting and encouraging each other, so much so that the batsmen couldn't hear the bowlers' warning 'Are you ready?' This made things more chaotic than usual but, as ever, the first rule of the game is 'have fun', and they were certainly doing that.

I talked a lot to the head groundsman, Fradrick, while helping him and his assistant roll the wicket with a massive roller built to be pulled by horses. He said that the last horse had died a few months ago. Apparently it went well with mealie, so now humans had to do the pulling and pushing. Until recently he had been a teacher at the local school, but the government had stopped paying the teachers, and at least as a groundsman he earned enough to feed his family. Just.

Unlike in apartheid South Africa, education was always good in Rhodesia for blacks as well as whites, which only reinforced the tragedy as Zimbabwe descended into chaos after the 2000 election. So much for the benefits of democracy – without Mugabe having to resort to scorched-earth policies to win the election, it's likely that Zimbabwe would have fared better.

I'd got to know Cyril well by now and I decided to break the golden rule that one should not talk politics. He was happy to oblige, in fact I think he'd been waiting for me ask about the situation. He was old enough to compare today's Zimbabwe with yesterday's Rhodesia, and admitted that in most respects life was better under Ian Smith's white regime in the 1960s and 1970s, even though most of that period was taken up by a vicious civil war and harsh trade sanctions. He didn't like Ian Smith, who was a white extremist, but he didn't like Mugabe either, who was a black extremist, and at least under Smith there was work, food, fuel and education.

The kids were having another good day even if I now wasn't. Feeling sad after my chats to Fradrick and Cyril, I decided I needed some quiet. At the end of play I bought a paper and strolled alone up Herbert Chitepo Street to the Bulldog Bar for a quiet drink. I passed many beggars on my way, mostly black, but also old white people too – too old to get out of Zimbabwe and, like the blacks, trapped in a descending spiral of despair.

I noticed that one of the ZCU coaches was following me, but thought nothing of it. I stopped to buy some beautiful carved wooden animals and even some 1950s postcards of Umtali, which looked like a paradise. Fifty yards back, the coach stopped too.

In the Bulldog Bar, I bought a Zambezi lager, and settled down in the corner to read my paper. The place was busy with locals enjoying a drink at the end of the working day. Then I looked up and saw my stalker, the ZCU coach. He was at the other end of the bar, pretending not to look at me. I remembered the advice the Foreign Office had given me. They were right – there is always someone from the government checking on you in Zimbabwe, and in my case it was this ZCU coach. I was suddenly terrified that Cyril had told him about our conversation. Finishing my drink nervously, I ordered another and, seeing that the stalker's was empty, I sent a drink across to him. He took it, smiled across the bar, and mouthed 'Cheers'. I drank up and left, but thankfully wasn't followed. Bribery – it gets you anything you want in Africa.

Because we were working only up until lunchtime there was time to look around and see if the Eastern Highlands deserved their reputation as a holiday paradise in the old days. The Bvumba mountains ('mountains of the mist'), could almost be in Scotland, except the mist refers to a heat haze, not rain. We played a round of golf at Leopard Rock, a beautiful course witnessing some truly dreadful play. Still, we could see why the Queen Mother said in the 1950s that 'there is nowhere more beautiful in Africa'. And I don't think she was even a golfer.

Manicaland is the name of the region, but the town of Manica itself is over the border in Mozambique. The Portuguese came to the region in 1569 looking for gold in them there hills. Over 300 years later, Cecil Rhodes wanted it too, so he pushed them out of Manicaland, although they kept the town itself. On the spurious grounds that Mozambique is a pretty good stamp to get in your passport, we paid our way through the customs post and hitched a lift to Manica in a truck.

The driver of the truck, an old Portuguese colonial called José de Silva, recommended a restaurant run by a pal of his, an old Rhodesia hand, and he joined us for lunch. Manica had obviously been a fabulous place, but everything apart from the restaurant was derelict. A full size swimming pool with a gantry of diving boards was empty, tennis courts were overgrown, and the roads were reverting to nature. The Portuguese had left 30 years previously in 1975, and it looked like they'd thrown away the key, leaving Manica as an unkempt 1970s throwback.

But lunch was good. We were the only customers that day, or probably that year, and our host Harry pulled out all the stops for us, with his finest wines and seafood. I didn't have any dollars or any Mozambican currency (meticais) but George surprised me by accepting a credit card, so I paid the bill of several hundred thousand meticais for six of us without any idea how much it was. Obviously Mozambique was suffering from inflation too, as £60 was the answer when my credit card statement arrived a month later. A fine man, Harry, and I hope his trade has picked up.

José and I had been talking business over lunch. Mozambique, like most of Africa, is resource rich but doesn't have the investment to take advantage of this. I guess because I'd been wafting about a sheaf of credit cards, José had marked me down as a potential investor and he suggested I buy into half a mountain he owned. 'We'll pass it on the way back to the border,' he said. 'It's full of gold.' Perhaps this was the gold his Portuguese forbear Francisco Barreto had been looking for in 1569, and the gold that eluded Cecil Rhodes in 1890? José's business card said Wolf Gold Mining Ltd., which certainly sounded good.

On the road back to the border we did indeed pass the mountain, which funnily enough was surrounded by a golden glow as the sun set behind it. However, I noticed that most of the people walking along the road, also heading for the border, were armed with what looked like AK47's slung nonchalantly on their shoulders. This put me off a bit, so José then suggested I invest instead in a port development on the coast in Nacala.

I did look into the proposals back home, and José sent me a pile of stuff to back them up. There's certainly a lot of money to be made in Africa, as the world cries out for raw materials, but you're either an entrepreneur or you're not. I'm not, but I hope that José becomes rich, because he made our day in Mozambique.

Norman and Cyril were waiting for us on the Zimbabwe side of the border, and said that if there had been any police to alert they would have done so, because what we'd just done – travelling unaccompanied and unarmed across the border to Manica and back – was seriously dangerous. 'People are killed every week on that road, it's bandit country.' They were right, but we hadn't half had a good time.

We said our farewells in Mutare. Norman had been a brilliant organiser. The coaches, even my stalker, who gave me a special hug, had expanded their repertoire and, most importantly, the kids from the Easterns Blind Cricket Club had become sportsmen, with a talent to be proud of.

In Harare there was time to look up some chums before our flight back. I'd met two white Zimbabweans, Bob and Patrick, in London and they were keen to show us their lives back home. Patrick Mavros is well-known in Africa, London and New York for his wonderful silver jewellery, often featuring representations of African wildlife. His great grandfather had been part of the Pioneer Column to what became Rhodesia, led by Cecil Rhodes in 1890. Patrick's love for the country was undimmed, despite the problems that had existed for practically the whole of his lifetime there. We looked around his workshops and he gave us each a beautiful little silver elephant. Then we had tea on the terrace of his fabulous property on the outskirts of town, looking out over a wooded valley full of wildlife. 'We're safe here,' he said. 'The house over there is owned by the Commander-in-Chief of the Zimbabwean Army;

he's a good friend of mine.' A useful friend to have in a tough country like Zimbabwe.

Patrick was amazed at what we'd come to his country to do, and wanted to help. We talked about the next Blind Cricket World Cup at Rawalpindi in Pakistan the coming year. 'Is there a trophy?' We said there wasn't. 'I'll make you one.' Sure enough, a year later the winners of the tournament, Pakistan, held aloft the Mavros Trophy, a magnificent creation in ebony with a pride of lions holding up a silver 'cricket ball' globe.

Bob was an endangered species in Zimbabwe – a white tobacco farmer. His father had given up and gone to live in South Africa, worn out by the struggle to keep the farm, a couple of hours north of Harare. Bob was a young man, a proud born-and-bred Zimbabwean, and was determined to carry it on. I'd been trying to get hold of him from Mutare with no luck, so had rung his mate in London to see if he could raise him. It worked and there was an explanation. 'I can't ring UK mobiles from Zimbabwe because the phone companies have no foreign exchange to pay for the overseas part of mobile calls.' He had also been suspicious. 'Who is Tom Rodwell? The name rings a bell. And why does he want me? Why can't you send me a female?' he had apparently replied to his chum.

Luckily, he was coming to town for the tobacco auctions, so he picked up me and Mikey from the Holiday Inn in Harare in the biggest pick-up truck I'd ever seen, straight out of Hollywood. Mikey wanted to go in the back, so we careered around Harare with him rolling around, shrieking and laughing at the same time. At the tobacco auctions, there wasn't much tobacco and there weren't many farmers. 'Five years ago this place would have been packed,' said Bob. 'But now there's only a few of us left.' Still, he sold his crop, which would give him enough money to buy next year's seed, if there was a next year.

On his farm the family had built a school and a health centre for his hundred-odd workers. It was those workers who had defended his farm from attack by the 'army veterans'. He said that the worst thing about the whole situation was that it made you a criminal. So many people had to be paid off in order for him to survive, from a few dollars for the lowly, to several thousand for the government people. Every week.

After the auction, Mikey and I had lunch with Bob and a friend of his who was also fascinated by what we'd been doing. He was Dean du Plessis, the world's only blind cricket commentator. I'd read about him in the *Daily Telegraph*; about how he hears the power and direction of the shot, and how he listens to the speed and spin of the ball, along with the player's exertions and their cries of elation or frustration. He senses the excitement – or otherwise – of the play on the cricket field and collates the scores with a computer-like memory. 'I'm generally spot-on or very close. I think I have a pretty big hard drive in my head,' he said. He didn't seem to think he was doing anything remarkable, just using his other more developed senses to give his radio audience an accurate and enthusiastic report of what was happening. But he was extraordinary – yet another extraordinary character in a country full of them.

That evening Bob was meeting up with some pals at the Epworth Balancing Rocks, a few miles out of Harare, to say cheerio to one of them. Charlie, another white Zimbabwean, was leaving home for England. The Rocks are famous both for what they are – enormous lumps of rock, hundreds of feet high, which balance on each other precariously but permanently – and for their familiarity, since they appear on all Zimbabwe's bank notes, so are also called the 'Bank Notes'.

It's become a custom to send emigrants off with a few beers by the Rocks, so we stopped off at a supermarket to get some Castle Lagers. The place was virtually empty of people and produce, but thankfully the beers were there for us. I paid for them with a Z$500 dollar note and got no change. Three years later, you could buy those same beers with no change from a similar note, still with a picture of the Rocks, and the same governor's signature, Dr G. Gono, but with the face value of Z$20,000,000,000 dollars. By that time, room service at our hotel in Harare for a club sandwich was the same: Z$20,000,000,000! Now that's what I call inflation.

We left Zimbabwe with mixed emotions. Despite the warnings of the Foreign Office and the ECB, nothing terrible had happened to us, and we'd succeeded in introducing a new version of cricket to both coaches and blind kids. But we feared for the future of all the people we'd met. Mugabe's regime is seriously awful and doing damage that will take generations to repair, if indeed it can ever be.

It was with some relief that we went through passport control to the relative safety of the departure lounge. Most departure lounges have a range of duty-free shops to take care of the last of your money, but in Harare there were only two: a music store and a second-hand bookshop, the first one I'd ever seen in an airport. Every airport should have one.

At the music store, I asked the girl what I should take back as a souvenir of Zimbabwe, and she immediately said 'Corruption' by Thomas Mapfumo. Mapfumo made his name by singing songs criticising the Ian Smith regime, but he'd realised that Mugabe was arguably worse, hence the 'Corruption' song. However, having been threatened with death more than once, he was now sensibly raging against the regime from the safety of the United States.

I could spend hours in second-hand bookshops, and nearly missed my flight because I was so engrossed. I bought a copy of *The Story of Rhodesian Sport, Volume One 1889 to 1935* by J. de L. Thompson, the 1935 original edition reprinted by Rhodesia Books in 1976. I read it on the flight back and discovered that 'Miss C. Rodwell, daughter of a former governor [was] the best lady swimmer the colony has produced'. The former governor was Cecil Hunter Rodwell, KCMG, GCMG, the main man between 1928 and 1934. Sounds a bit posh to have been a relative of mine, but you never know.

Our flight back had to stop in Cairo, as there was not sufficient fuel in Harare to complete the journey. Would we ever get home? Well, we did, and a few weeks later I got a letter from Zimbabwe, with stamps to the value of Z$66,000 on the brown paper envelope. It was from Godfrey Zimunya, the assistant groundsman at Mutare Sports Club, whom I'd helped to push the roller:

Dear Mr T. Rodwell,

Here life is getting too hard. Please can you help me with anything you can afford? I will be happy to receive any kind of help from you.

Thank you, Goodbye,
Yours Faithful,
Godfrey Zimunya.

He summed up Zimbabwe. I'd seen too many beggars in Mutare to ignore this plea, so I didn't.

Our first real work in Africa had been tough and, to be honest, upsetting. We had witnessed at first hand the contrast between the essentially decent Zimbabwean, whether black or white, and what he was confronted by: a regime wilfully destroying a once-rich country. However, Nicholas Muramagi from the UN conference in Zambia had been back in touch with his plans, which were starting in Uganda. It would be interesting to 'compare and contrast' its situation, as that country once harboured another despot every bit as bad as Mugabe, Idi Amin.

11

UGANDA – RAID ON ENTEBBE

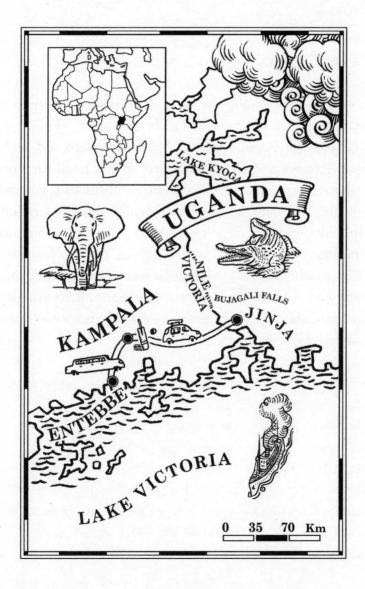

AFRICA IS ALWAYS FULL OF SURPRISES. The Ugandan capital is Kampala, but its airport is at Entebbe, which is about as far away from Kampala as Luton airport is from London. I'd heard of the airport only through the movie *Raid on Entebbe*, the true story of Israeli forces rescuing hostages from a hijacked plane, and was expecting an airport about the size of Luton. But Entebbe from a few thousand feet up was like one of those shots of hundreds of dead American planes in the Mojave desert, but when we landed the planes were all in service. Entebbe serves as the UN base for all its activities in the region, supplying over 60,000 UN personnel who are trying to solve the chaos in the Congo, Burundi and Darfur. Peace is worth fighting for – in just one of the conflicts in Uganda's neighbour, the Democratic Republic of Congo, it's estimated that over 5 million people have died since 1998, making it the bloodiest conflict since 1945.

The second surprise at Entebbe was that we weren't met by my mate from the departure lounge at Livingstone airport, Nicholas Muramagi, but by a fleet of limos with darkened windows that whisked us to our hotel in Kampala. The drivers said that they'd been arranged by one of the president's advisors, and, not wanting to be yet another grim statistic in the region, we didn't argue.

And Kampala was yet another surprise. Built, like Rome (and indeed Sheffield), on seven hills, it certainly wasn't a ramshackle African backwater, but a buzzy and busy metropolis that seemed to know where it was going. Even when Stanley, of Livingstone and Stanley fame, passed through in 1875, he found the capital of the local Bugandans to be 'a well ordered city of some 40,000 souls'. Despite ex-President

Amin's best efforts between 1971 and 1979, it still seemed in pretty good order. As indeed did modern Uganda in general. Churchill described it as 'the Pearl of Africa' and on first impressions the pearl had kept most of its lustre.

One of Amin's first acts had been to throw out most of the Asians, who were economically very active. Many ended up in my home town of Leicester, so much so that in September 1972, Leicester City Council put an advert in the *Uganda Argus* urging Ugandan Asians not to come to Leicester: 'In your own interests and those of your family you should accept the advice of the Uganda Resettlement Board and not come to Leicester.' Some ad. So I thought I'd better not tell anyone that I was from Leicester.

The final surprise was our hotel – at No. 1 Nile Avenue (what a great address) – the Speke Hotel, named after the explorer who was the first white man to discover the source of the White Nile in 1859. (This claim was hotly disputed for years by his fellow explorer Sir Richard Burton.) The Speke Hotel was a wonderful survivor of colonial days, with whirring fans cooling its mahogany walls, but the surprise was the astonishing nightclub next door, the Rock Bar. *Bradt's Guide* gives a clue, saying: 'The attached nightclub can be disturbingly noisy'. This turned out to be a tremendous understatement – it was like living next door to Sodom and Gomorrah.

Nicholas met us there with a massive smile and another legendary handshake, which must be an African thing. He said he didn't normally frequent places like the Rock Bar because he was about to get married. We ordered a round of Nile beers and admired the scenery. I wondered whether Nicholas's protestations were more because his boss, Jasper, the general secretary of Uganda's National Council of Sports was with him, rather than any concerns relating to his imminent marriage, but that's none of my business. We enjoyed a great reunion and drank a toast to the five dollars I had given him in Livingstone departure lounge, which had brought us to Uganda.

Then my mobile rang. It's always a worry when the mobile rings at the start of a trip. Trouble at home? Someone ill? It was hard to hear over the Congo classics being belted out in the Rock Bar, but John Nagenda's bellowing patrician tones could cut through most noise, and I discovered that he was the reason for our darkened window cavalcade from Entebbe to Kampala.

I hadn't seen or heard from Nagenda for over 25 years. Linked to the Bugandan royals, he'd spent most of the 1970s in exile in England to escape the attention of Amin, but famously played for East Africa in the first Cricket World Cup in England in 1975. *Wisden* has their team photo, which has only two black faces in it, one of whom was Nagenda, and two white faces, one of whom was the ex-England all-rounder Derek Pringle's late father. The rest are Asian, and I wondered how many had survived the attentions of Amin.

Looking at the scores, Nagenda played only once, taking a creditable one for 50 off nine overs versus New Zealand, for whom Glenn Turner scored 171. But he was a good player (that's Nagenda as well as Turner) and was much sought after in English wandering cricket whenever he was around, especially by the Stoics CC.

I was running my cricket team back then, and he played for me a few times during a period when he was editing a paper called *The Club Cricketer*. Looking back at the scorebooks, the last game he played for us was at Hurlingham, when Arun Lal, the ex-India Test player opened for us and scored 145 out of our total of 207 for seven. He would have got more, but Nagenda ran him out while on his way to a statuesque 14 not out. But we had more lunches than matches, talking about playing rather than actually doing it, which I find is generally more fun.

In those days, he was always short of money, and often paid for his share of lunch by offering dead-cert tips on horses to win that afternoon. As they rarely won, all this did was make the lunches even more expensive, and to compensate for the theoretical deficit over one summer he offered to make me Uganda's sports minister when his tribe got back in power. I was rather tickled by this, but asked if I could do the job based in Hertfordshire. He readily agreed to this, as he said he planned to be their foreign minister while being based in St John's Wood.

After Amin's fall from power, Nagenda went back to Uganda and I never heard from him again. Indeed, a few years later, I was somewhat miffed to read about a sports minister who was obviously a local chap being appointed by President Museveni, one of Nagenda's party. Knowing I was off to Uganda, I'd managed to get a message to Nagenda via the Stoics' network and, unbeknown to me, it was he who'd fixed the limos.

He explained that he was a bit busy, as African leaders were piling into Kampala for the swearing-in of President Museveni after another election victory, which Nagenda, as the president's advisor on media affairs (think a black Peter Mandelson or Alastair Campbell), had had a lot to do with. He was worried about the official dinner, because rather foolishly he'd just written a damning article about several of the assembled dignitaries in his weekly column in the local paper, *New Vision*. His byline in the paper described him as 'Informed, Controversial and Provocative', which, while noble, in Central Africa doesn't normally lend itself to a long and happy life. Nevertheless, 'God willing', he said he'd see us all the following evening over the road in the bar at the Sheraton Hotel where the dinner was being held.

The following morning, we discovered what Nicholas had been up to since we met in Zambia. He'd organised for a total of 40 disabled potential cricketers and 18 potential cricket coaches to descend on the Lugogo Sports Centre in Kyadondo on the outskirts of Kampala. They'd been bussed in from the four regions of Uganda, a journey of many hours on terrible roads for most, and for some a dangerous one, given the tension on the Congo border to the east, and a civil war raging in the north against Joseph Kony's Lord's Resistance Army.

This is yet another little-known African war, which over a 20-year period has killed tens of thousands and maimed many more. When you first hear the name of those fighting and don't know the detail, I'm ashamed to say it's easy to laugh it off as maybe a group of disgruntled MCC members upset at not getting their favourite Ashes seats at Lord's, but the reality is terrifying. Kony maims as much as he kills, amputating limbs, and concentrates on the young. He is still at large and a massive worldwide campaign called Kony 2012 has recently been launched to bring attention to this issue and demand that the international community help bring him to justice.

Several of the assembled players were victims of Kony, but they couldn't wait to get stuck into the new game that Nicholas had told them about. None had wheelchairs or proper crutches, because both were too expensive, but all had found their own way to get around, some just shuffling around on their torsos, others with handmade crutches made from local wood. One of the stars was Susie, who'd lost both her legs and yet was incredibly mobile. She always wore vibrant clothes with a matching turban, which, combined with her permanent smile, lit up the morning. Mikey made a fuss of her, and they used to dance together on the grass to Mikey's version of Wham's 'Wake Me Up Before You Go Go', 'Wake Me Up Before Lugogo', which was always worth a cheap laugh.

The Lugogo facility was excellent, apparently opened by the Queen in the 1950s when Uganda was still a colony. A big indoor hall provided shelter from the frequent rains, and the outdoor pitch had just been renovated with help from the MCC, who'd been there on a recent tour. Although most of the Asian cricket influence had been snuffed out by Amin, local Africans had taken to the game, encouraged by people such as King Freddie of Buganda and John Nagenda, who'd learnt the game in England, and Robert Kisubi, from the Uganda Cricket Board. The board had provided some of the coaches, among them terrific woman cricketers from the Uganda national team.

One of the potential coaches, Simon Ojok, had come all the way from Gulu, in the far north of the country. This was a town overwhelmed by people who'd come over the border from the Sudan to escape yet another African war in Darfur. On the map, the border crossing north of Gulu at Nimule says 'may be closed, inquire current situation', but thousands of asylum seekers cross every year hoping for a more peaceful life. Sadly they do so not realising that they are entering the heartland of Joseph Kony's Lord's Resistance Army.

Simon was a tall, very thin, young man, about eighteen years old, who looked more like a Masai than a Bugandan. He wore thick glasses and was almost blind, due to a poor diet and constant bouts of malaria. Despite this, he was desperate to improve himself and those around him, and he'd set his heart on becoming a sports coach and going to Makerere University in Kampala.

To help persuade the enthusiastic young people assembled at Lugogo that they could play sport, despite their various disabilities, we'd brought Kerryn along with us. A totally blind Welshman, he was a double international, for the GB Blind Football team, who play at the Paralympics, and for the England Blind Cricket team. In all the reference books, it says that Willie Watson and Arthur Milton were the last two people to play both international cricket and football, back in the 1950s, but the answer should be Kerryn Seal, in the first decade of the 21st century – even if he is Welsh.

The players were split up into two groups, the blind and the disabled, with Kerryn astonishing the watching group with his demonstration of powerful batting. Mikey was the hero to the disabled group, being able to get even those with missing limbs to bat and bowl successfully. Those without legs such as Susie were allocated runners and soon a semblance of a cricket match was taking place. I watched from the steep slope overlooking the ground. The players were enjoying themselves, and a few interested spectators were looking on. Whatever you're doing in Africa, in no time at all there's an inquisitive gathering. Many of this particular crowd had been boxing in the sports hall and were fascinated by the quick achievements of our group of players and coaches. Soon we were all talking cricket, and the whole scene started to remind me of an African Arundel, with a wonderful view of the cricket ground below framed by massive trees and hills in the distance.

A break for lunch saw the boxers helping out the cricketers and the cricketers supporting the boxers, one of whom was a tiny boy called Jimmy whose father was African champion and who wanted to be the same. Mikey's old tyro Tony Joseph had missed some of our recent trips, and it was good to have him back on this one. Tony had done some boxing in his time and sparred with Jimmy, an eight-year-old against Tony's 30-something, which was a worry until Tony took a dive and hailed Jimmy as the new champion. There's a long history of Ugandan boxing champions. I remember Kampala's John 'The Beast' Mugabi winning a silver at the 1980 Olympics, and then a few years later giving 'Marvellous' Marvin Hagler the fight and the fright of his life, so maybe Jimmy will make the grade too.

Uganda is crazy about sport and since we'd exhausted our cricketers for the day, when I noticed crowds turning up at the Kyadondo rugby ground next door I decided to wander down to see who was playing. I discovered it was 'the big one': Uganda v Kenya, playing for the Elgon Cup. Now, there are lots of famous cups played for in rugby. The Calcutta Cup for England v Scotland and the Bledisloe Cup for Australia v New Zealand, for example. However, it was soon apparent that these pale into insignificance against the Elgon Cup. Mount Elgon is on the border between Uganda and Kenya, and each year the two teams play home and away to decide 'who will claim the mountain'.

The infamous ex-President Amin was a big man and a big rugby fan. He played in the 1960s and had encouraged the game in the 1970s. A British officer who'd played against him described him as 'a splendid type and a good player, but virtually bone from the neck up, and needs things explained in words of one letter'. A bit like most of the forwards I've played with and against.

There followed the most brutal game of rugby I'd ever witnessed. As a kicking fly-half, I've been in quite a few tough matches. Playing in South Africa for the Sinners RFC was no fun, and Australia wasn't much better, and in the old days Leicester Tigers v Coventry was always a blood bath. But none of these could compare with the Elgon Cup. At half time it was 0-0, and there'd been more boxing than rugby, so it was a good job they enjoyed both sports. Kenya then scored a disputed try under the posts, which led to more boxing, but also to a 0-7 scoreline. Uganda emptied its bench to replace all their injured players and went for one final desperate, but thankfully successful, push. It was 5-7, with a tricky conversion to come. Success: 7-7. Honours even and animosity forgotten, everyone back to the bar, just like in England. (Later in the year, I heard that in the away fixture Uganda had won 22-20, which sounded like another tough encounter.)

I wanted to get a Uganda rugby shirt for my son. I wanted one for myself really, because Uganda's colours are the same as Watford FC's (or is it the other way round), but old blokes look so sad in replica shirts, so I only bought the one. The guy in charge of the paraphernalia around the Uganda team was a Kiwi (had to be) called Cam McLeay, an explorer who ran a tourism business based on the Nile.

All along its length the Nile is called 'The River of Life' and it has fascinated explorers for a century and a half. Cam said that John Hanning Speke reckoned he'd found the source of the Nile in what he called Lake Victoria, but his publicity-conscious explorer rival Burton would have none of it. In a case as sad as that between Scott and Amundsen at the South Pole, in 1864, a full five years after Speke's discovery, Burton challenged Speke to a public debate in Bath to settle the matter. However, the day before the debate, Speke, out game shooting, accidentally shot himself while climbing over a wall. Even though Speke was later proved right, there is still controversy as to whether it was an accident, or whether the stress of the five years' argument had been too much for the poor chap.

Tim Jeal is the expert on these great explorers and tells their tales in a wonderful recent book *Explorers of the Nile*, while Alan Moorhead's books on the White and Blue Niles from the 1960s are now regarded as classics and great reads.

I'd never met an explorer before, and Cam was full of his latest exploits, where he'd made the first-ever descent of the White Nile to the Mediterranean by raft, and discovered that it was 107km longer than previously thought, making it 6,718km long. But, just as Speke found out, exploration is a dangerous business – Cam lost one of his men to the Lord's Resistance Army en route, so River of Death might be a more accurate description than River of Life. Despite this, he insisted that while in Uganda we must do some Nile exploration of our own, so we arranged to meet in a couple of days to see what rafting was like.

With the story of Speke and the Nile still ringing in my ears, I went back to 'his' hotel to get ready to see my old pal Nagenda. As it was over 25 years since I'd seen him I thought it was unlikely that we'd recognise each other. In fact when we trooped into the Sheraton's Rhino Bar at the appointed hour it was deserted. The barmaid came across to us: 'Are you gentlemen waiting for Mr Nagenda?' Of course we said we were. 'Well, he's sorry to be late because of all the African leaders here, but he'll be along shortly and would like you to drink this before he arrives.' She plonked a large bottle of Smirnoff down on our table, and I suddenly remembered that Nagenda was a vodka man, and probably wasn't far away.

Indeed he wasn't – after twenty minutes or so, a great *basso profundo* shout of 'Rodwell!' echoed across the empty bar, and there was a big old black man, dressed from head to toe in a flowing white robe, topped off with a headdress made out of the head of a stuffed leopard. It was Nagenda.

'Sorry about all this, old boy. Much prefer a nice Savile Row suit myself, but we've got to be all African today, what with all the leaders in town.' At their official dinner upstairs, he'd been sat between Presidents Thabo Mbeki from South Africa and the infamous Robert Mugabe from Zimbabwe, I guess because 'U' for Uganda comes between 'S' and 'Z'. It had been difficult for him to make his excuses, although he said that the other two were big pals and wouldn't miss him.

Their loss was our gain, as we were able to relive our time together all those years ago. Nagenda had become a big cheese in Uganda because of his support for President Museveni, and although I hadn't been able to contact him directly before travelling, he knew all about our trip as both the British and Ugandan governments had checked us out with him. We had so much to talk about, but in the end I just had to ask why I'd never been made Ugandan sports minister, as he'd promised.

'Yes, sorry about that, old boy. These things happen. Politics is a tough old world you know. Some you win and some you lose. And in your case you lost.' At this he guffawed so much that his leopard's head almost toppled off, and he ordered more vodka, having left my putative political career in ruins. But he did pay the bill, although I've a suspicion it went on one of the visiting African countries' tabs.

The following morning there was great excitement at Lugogo, as there'd been two significant articles in the *New Vision* newspaper, which we brought along to show everyone. The first was about the British High Commission's support for the programme, under the headline 'Step Up To Bat For Disabled Young People In Uganda', with a picture of all the coaches and players. This was the first time any of them had been in the papers, and all clamoured for a copy, so I went off to buy 40, which made the day of the paperboy by the side of the main road.

So much of the effect of programmes like these is in making the young people feel good about themselves and the article was a wonderful example of this. The coaches were proud too, as the article stressed that it was they who were going to carry on the work after we'd gone. One of them, Francis Odongo, was disabled himself, balancing his withered leg with a stick as big as himself, and using it to be as mobile as the best of us. He'd come from Iganga, about 80 miles east of Kampala, and was determined to learn as much as possible because he planned to set up a youth disabled club which, apart from sport, would also teach tree planting, floriculture and water harvesting. I never found out exactly what water harvesting was, but lack of drinking water is one of the biggest problems facing Uganda (and Africa in general) so Francis was perhaps ahead of the game in every sense of the word. He was fascinated by the scoring system in cricket, and I promised to send him a cricket scorebook when I got home as my contribution to his ferocious desire to better himself and those around him.

The other excitement in the *New Vision* was an article about the movie *The Last King of Scotland*. This was based on Giles Foden's book about some of the more bizarre aspects of ex-President Amin's life. It was being shot in Uganda, starring the Hollywood actor Forest Whitaker. The previous evening, Nagenda had told us that he was acting as technical advisor to the movie, a role which, though lucrative, still brought back some painful memories for him. There was a picture in the paper of Forest Whitaker, dressed as Amin, and he bore a startling resemblance to Mikey, being massive, black and good looking. Mikey naturally played up to this – he insisted on being called 'Mr Whitaker' all day and instead of starting each aspect of the game with the word 'play', called 'action' instead. Mikey's performance that day was worth an Oscar, one which Whitaker himself duly got a couple of years later for his performance.

I'm not a teacher, but getting everyone to have fun while learning at the same time is a gift that Mikey possesses, one which comes to him entirely intuitively. The importance of getting this balance right is a subject entirely absent from every cricket coaching book that I've ever seen, more's the pity.

While one of Mikey's more uproarious impressions of President Amin aka Forest Whitaker was going on, John Hamilton from the High Commission popped down to introduce himself to us and discuss arrangements for the final day's presentation. He wasn't in any way from the Foreign Office's central casting department, being an amusing young Scotsman who'd dropped out of university, married a black girl from London, and got a job by saying the service needed people like him as well as the Oxbridge stereotypes.

He said he'd come back to the hotel that evening to show us some of the real Kampala, as opposed to the Rock Bar, which while at first amusing was starting to lose its attraction, as it closed for business at about the same time as when we left the hotel to work, with a flurry of boda boda motorbike taxis screaming down Nile Avenue taking its last customers home.

The real Kampala that John wanted to show us was an outdoor music venue called Club Obligatto, where the resident band was the Afrigo Band, a Ugandan institution since 1976, during the height (or perhaps depths) of Amin's rule. Despite the political nature of some of their music, they'd survived his regime and although 30-year veterans, they played their own invention, Uganda reggae, with the enthusiasm of *X-Factor* contestants. The lead singer was Juanita Kawalya. I don't know whether her first name really came from the Spanish, but the music had echoes of Cuba in it, maybe from the time when the Cubans were supporting African revolutions in the 1970s.

Mikey, always proud of his Jamaican roots, at first thought they had a cheek calling their music 'reggae', but he soon warmed to it, and joined Juanita on stage for a duet that astounded the locals, as he introduced himself as Forest Whitaker, the great Hollywood star. A real all-rounder.

Despite an early-hours finish to the music, we were all on parade for the final presentations to the players and coaches the following morning. We wanted the coaches to be as big a part of the presentation as possible, and as John had brought his boss along to do the honours, I asked Simon Ojok to introduce him. This he duly did, as 'His Majesty' Jeremy Macadie, which certainly amused us. 'His Majesty' the High Commissioner himself didn't seem to find it quite as funny.

T-shirts and certificates were proudly accepted by the players, and the coaches got smart tracksuits. We did our bit by handing out second-hand laptops we'd brought with us to each of the four regions, so that they'd be able to keep in touch with Nicholas and his team in Kampala. While many in Africa have mobile phones, computers are much rarer and really do transform lives in countries where communication is difficult.

Nicholas was rightly as proud as punch of everyone's efforts and the results achieved, especially as everything was witnessed by the assembled high-level Brits, Ugandans and the media. Afterwards he insisted on taking us to his favourite rooftop bar on the outskirts of Kampala to thank us and talk about the next steps. First, though, he rang the bar to check they had electricity that day. Like water, electricity is an ongoing problem in Uganda and they were operating one day on, one day off in certain areas of town. Luckily, power was on, so we were on.

While the coaching programme was going on, Nicholas had been busy again with his pals from the neighbouring countries that he'd met at the conference way back in Zambia. He announced to us that because things had been such a success in Uganda he wanted to extend the work to Rwanda, Burundi, Tanzania and maybe Kenya. He didn't seem to like the Kenyans much, which may be a common Ugandan thing, if the rugby match we'd watched a few days previously was anything to go by. He also said he wanted us to come back and help him, to which the answer had to be 'Sure, why not?'

Cam McLeay had been back in touch, insisting that before we left Uganda we had to experience the Nile, his Nile. He'd organised two trips for us, one on Lake Victoria and the other rafting down the Nile through the Bujagali Falls.

Lake Victoria was beautiful and uneventful, apart from having to be pulled back onto the boat from swimming because Nile crocodiles had been sighted heading our way. Apparently they are normally harmless, preferring fish, but they didn't look harmless to me as they approached with their teeth glistening in the sun. I checked later in *Bradt's Guide*, which disarmingly states that Nile crocodiles 'will also prey on drinking and swimming mammals where the opportunity presents itself, dragging their victim underwater until it drowns, then storing it under a submerged log or tree until it has decomposed sufficiently for them to eat.' Being a swimming mammal myself, I was pleased to have got back onto the boat before becoming dinner.

The Bujagali Falls were something else. They are a series of seven rapids downstream from the town of Jinja, not far from where the Nile empties out of Lake Victoria on its long journey to the Mediterranean. Three of the rapids are rated five, which is the highest and most dangerous category.

I remembered Joseph Conrad's *Heart of Darkness*, which is a terrifying story about a journey down another great African river, the Congo. We weren't too far away from the Congo, and recollecting the unpleasant happenings in Conrad's book perhaps wasn't the best preparation for a nerve-racking trip, particularly when I'm not that keen on extreme sports, either. Lines in the book such as 'The brown current ran swiftly out of the heart of darkness, bearing us down towards the sea' did nothing for my confidence. Graham Greene wrote frighteningly about the Congo too in his *Congo Journal* – yet more unsettling images for me to dwell on.

Cam said that we'd got to traverse the rapids while they lasted, because there was a plan to dam the river there in order to provide much-needed electricity, a project which would drown the rapids. 'A dam bad idea,' he said (the old jokes are the best), but I guess you would if you ran a company which organised rafting trips on the Nile. He delegated his best pilot rafter, Paolo, to look after us. He was from Peru, and said he'd canoed for Peru in the Olympics, which was reassuring, though I was still terrified at the prospect of rafting down the world's most dangerous rapids.

He asked if we had any medical or personal conditions that might affect our participation. I was first up. 'Well, I'm an asthmatic and have got an artificial hip.'

'OK,' said Paolo. 'That's fine.'

'I can't swim,' said Mikey.

'Also fine,' said Paolo.

'And I'm blind,' said Kerryn.

'You mean really blind?' asked Paolo.

'Yes,' said Kerryn.

'But can you swim?'

'Yes,' answered Kerryn.

'Good. Let's go.'

So it seemed that if you were both blind *and* a non-swimmer Paolo might not let you down the Falls, but otherwise you were OK. The briefing was good. We were given our life jackets and our positions on the boat, and told not to worry if we fell out of the raft, which could happen, because the safety boat would pick us up.

Down we paddled, through the first rapid, which was easy, and then the first level five rapid, which was OK, though I had never been in a boat travelling so fast before, let alone one without an engine, piloted by a Peruvian. Nothing against Peruvians, of course. At the next set of rapids, however, it wasn't third time lucky. This level five rapid tipped both me and Kerryn out of the boat. It seemed like the end. I thought about my late parents, wife and son while I was thrown around in the depths of the Nile like an old pair of socks in a washing machine.

Paolo had briefed us on what to do if we fell out: 'Count to ten, slowly, then if you haven't surfaced, count to ten again, and so on.' After counting 32, I surfaced. Out of breath and exhausted, I could see the safety boat in the distance, pulling in another drowned rat. It was Kerryn. Then they came for me, pulled me out of the water and dumped me back in the raft, with another four sets of rapids to endure.

Finally we'd done it – made it through the rest of the rapids intact. With everyone safely back on board, we broke for lunch on a small island in the middle of the Nile. Paolo then hushed everyone. 'Gentlemen, I hope you all enjoyed your trip down the world's most dangerous rapids, but more important than that I just want to say that Kerryn here is the bravest man I've ever met. He is the first blind person to raft down the Bujagali Falls, and if the dam gets built, he will be the last. Well done, Kerryn.' All applauded. There was no mention at all of me and my asthma and hip, though.

Then suddenly Mikey screamed: 'A snake!' *Bradt's Guide* had warned ominously that 'all manner of venomous snakes occur in Uganda'. Although this wasn't very big, it was rising up about two foot, only yards away, and puffing out its throat. Luckily, Paolo grabbed a paddle and smashed it across the snake's head. He then said that even though the Bujagali Rapids seemed dangerous they weren't really, but that puff adders really were, and that the one he'd just killed could easily have ruined our lunch.

Nicholas came with us on our journey back to Entebbe airport. He told us all about the plans he'd made for his wedding, which I'd completely forgotten about. I asked him what he'd like for a wedding present and he said: 'Some smart shoes – got to look my best.' So I put a note in my diary to remind me. Despite the excitement of the forthcoming nuptials, he was already bubbling with ideas about how he was going to get the best of the Ugandan coaches down to Rwanda, which is on the south-west border, so that they could start spreading the project across the region. He said his government was keen to be seen as helping its neighbours. Our discussions with the British High Commission had also suggested that they might help, so although I'd not been looking forward to a final bone-crunching handshake from Nicholas, the smile that accompanied it took away some of the pain, as did his final words – 'See you in Rwanda.'

There are some good as well as some sad postscripts to our work in Uganda. I'd become friendly with Simon Ojok and he'd asked me, in the nicest possible way, if I could help him get through Makerere University in Kampala. At the time my son was just about to start his studies at Birmingham University so it was a subject close to my heart. I trusted Simon, and agreed to help out. Three years later, he sent me the following email:

'I am happy because God has made my life that way. From the son of a peasant farmer to a boy of success. From a poor family to the university. From being an orphan to being a professional. From a few friends to international friends like in UK. All this was possible through hard work and God blessing, which manifested on 21.01.09 at midday from Makerere University. Started by the Dean of Faculty of Arts reading the names of 305 students who had qualified for the award of degree in Bachelor of Development Studies and the name Simon Ojok appeared at number 235, then I stood up where I was seated in a chair also labelled Simon Ojok. And I walked out to the Freedom Square to take my photos then go to the bus park and travel back home. All in all I was happy and still happy. Bye, Simon.'

I like to think in a small way we'd helped Simon start to believe in himself, and to help others in a similar situation to himself. Francis Odongo had also delivered. He sent me a note saying that he'd started his Arams Youth Disabled Club and that it was doing well, including the mysterious water harvesting. And Nicholas and the Uganda Cricket Association were delighted when word was sent that the ICC had given Uganda the award for being the most innovative country for promoting cricket for persons with disability.

All this wonderful news was tempered by my seeing on the news in July 2010 that two bomb blasts at Kampala Rugby Club, where I'd met Cam McLeay, had killed 74 people, apparently as retribution for Ugandan troops being involved in peacekeeping duties in Somalia.

Such a beautiful country deserves better.

12

RWANDA – FROM CRICKET TO THE COMMONWEALTH

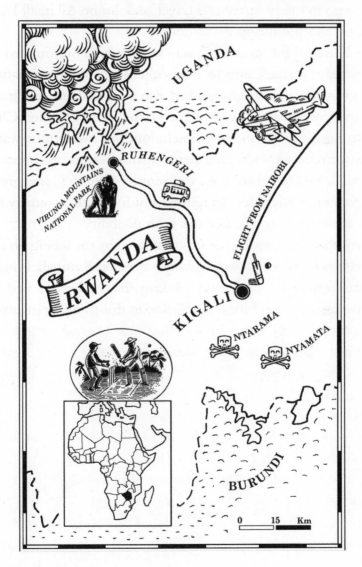

I VAGUELY REMEMBERED Rwanda and Burundi from my adolescent stamp collection. You could buy the stamps in job lots for pocket money. They were multicoloured, when ours were much more monochrome; they featured butterflies, birds and animals, when ours had only kings and queens; and they were so big that one doubted if they were ever used on envelopes.

Then, in 1994, these two 'unknown' countries were suddenly in the limelight on BBC News, as Fergal Keane reported on a tragedy unfolding day by day. We notice disasters in countries we know something about, but this African disaster seemed to creep up on us without our knowing. In fact it had been a hundred years in the making.

In the 'Scramble for Africa' in the late 19th century, a resurgent newly united Germany had grabbed a big piece of land that they called German East Africa; it was squeezed between King Leopold of Belgium's Congo and British East Africa. The British managed to grab back part of that land, Uganda and Zanzibar, by swapping them for the island of Heligoland, a small rocky outcrop that the Germans wanted to protect both their growing navy at Hamburg, and the entrance to the Keil canal. It was as if some giant card game was being arrogantly played out in the capitals of Europe, with regions of Africa as the stakes.

The Germans, using their newly created 'science' of eugenics, started to categorise the population of part of their new territory into Tutsis and Hutus, with the supposedly finer features of the Tutsis granting them preferential treatment. At the end of the First World War, the Germans lost their new empire and, as Thomas Pakenham states in his wonderful book *The Scramble for Africa*, 'Belgium was thrown a picturesque bone: Rwanda-Burundi, hidden away beside the mountains of the moon'.

Sadly, the Belgians also embraced eugenics with enthusiasm and thus still favoured the minority Tutsi population. After a hurried independence in the early 1960s, the Hutus started to get their own back with a series of mini genocides of the Tutsis, which prompted many to flee north to refugee camps over the border in Uganda.

That was the background of our driver Philip, a Tutsi, who picked us up from Kigali airport to take us to our hotel. He had been a bright boy, the brightest in the family. His parents wanted the best for him, so they encouraged him to go to Uganda as a teenager to get a better education. While in Uganda, over time he became part of a different sort of family, that of the Rwanda Patriotic Front (RPF). Led by Laurent Kabila, their avowed aim was to return to Rwanda to avenge the deaths of their fellow Tutsis over 40 years of Hutu rule, and create a new anglicised country.

Now was not the time to hear Philip's story, as he wanted to get us quickly to the hotel where he hoped to have news from Nicholas Muramagi, our friend from Uganda who was setting up the programme. On arrival, there was no word from him yet. 'Maybe tomorrow,' said Philip, 'but meanwhile enjoy the hotel, it's the Milles Collines, one of Rwanda's most famous.' Indeed it was. It was the very *Hotel Rwanda* that featured in the eponymous 2005 movie, which brought the true horror of the 1994 genocide to life. The brave manager of the hotel, Paul Rusesabagina, a Hutu married to a Tutsi, saved over 1200 Tutsi lives by refusing to give in to the Hutu militia. His story was published under the title *An Ordinary Man*, but he was surely anything but.

Wherever you go in Rwanda, there is no escaping the genocide. To some extent the same is true of Israel. Tim Butcher has written about the Rwanda region in *Blood River* and compares the two countries, calling Rwanda 'another small country of people driven by the memory of mass murder'. In Rwanda, however, the history is more recent and therefore even more raw.

With still no word from Nicholas, who was driving down from Uganda, on the first morning we went to the British embassy for a briefing. We were greeted by a homely pot of Earl Grey tea from the ambassador, who gave us a much less homely description of the recent history and ethnography of Rwanda. Obviously most of this concerned the Hutus and Tutsis, but he also introduced a third group, the pygmies, who were, he said, 'surprisingly tall', something which always amused him.

The now president of Rwanda, Laurent Kabila, had recently expelled the French ambassador, closed down the Lycee, Le Monde, the French Cultural Centre and Radio France International. This suggested that there had been another element to the genocide – the goal of preserving a French-speaking country in the face of the insurgent RPF who had been brought up in anglophone Uganda.

Kabila claimed that he had evidence that, at the time of the genocide, layers of the French government from the then president, François Mitterand, downwards knew a little too much about the Hutus' plans, including details such as the recent importation of over half a million machetes (cheaper than guns). It must be said that these allegations were strenuously denied.

Having spent time at school in France, I know how proud the French are of their language. It concerns them that, for instance, there are more French speakers in Rwanda's neighbour Congo than there are in France, so maybe the thought of losing hitherto francophone Rwanda to *perfide albion* might have been a factor in France's attitude.

The recent expulsion of the French had put Britain centre stage, which had made the ambassador 'frightfully busy', but he was all in favour of the cricket project, and invited us back for a soirée at the end of the week. Cricket, he felt, could be another way to help turn Rwanda into an anglicised country, the game being part of another great game — the end game of Rwanda becoming a member of the British Commonwealth. If one looks at the polyglot constituent countries in our Commonwealth, cricket, second perhaps only to the Queen, is the glue that holds it all together. OK, I know there's Canada where it is not so popular, but they do play a bit there, and Bradman famously said that the most beautiful ground he'd ever played on was in Stanley Park, Vancouver. Having been there myself, I must say, he could well have been right.

So, to hasten Rwanda's entry into the Commonwealth, the rapid development of cricket there became an important agenda item. English had appeared on Rwanda's banknotes in 2004. Now it was the turn of cricket to be used to further cement the policies of the British government, and we were being used to execute those policies. A strange honour, but one which with Nicholas's help we were happy to have a go at.

Cricket had been introduced into the country in 2000 by Tutsis returning from Uganda, as well as by the obligatory

South Asian fanatics. There was now a cricket ground, the Kicukiro Oval, at a school on the outskirts of Kigali, shared by the five teams. One of these teams, the Right Guards, was mainly Brits and Rwandans, while the remainder were Asian sides, including the equally wonderfully named Young Tigers.

Philip picked us up to take us back to the hotel, but insisted on going via a bookshop. I'd been pummelling him with questions about Rwanda's recent history and I think he reckoned a book might shut me up. Somehow it seemed strange to find a smart bookshop in a country recently on its knees, but the Ikirezi bookshop on the Avenue de la Paix was a model of its kind, the sort that every English neighbourhood used to have. I read the other day that there are now more pound shops in England than bookshops. No wonder the libraries are closing and a fifth of our kids can't read properly.

Philip recommended *Un Dimanche a la Piscine a Kigali* by Gil Courtemanche, a novel about the events in 1994 at the Hotel des Milles Collines, with a photograph of the derelict swimming pool taken that year on the front cover. It seemed very odd pulling up a lounger by that same pool, now renovated and inviting, ordering an ice cold Primus beer, and settling down to read about what had happened almost twenty years before on the very spot where I was lying.

Dinner followed at dusk, and, since there was still no sign of Nicholas, the hotel suggested that there was some good music at the nearby Nyira Rock Cafe. Actually, we could already hear it pounding in the distance. Thankfully, the atmosphere wasn't quite as 'Decline and Fall of the Roman Empire' as the Speke Hotel's Rock Bar. There was something of an African karaoke affair going on, with one of the contestants murdering 'Rwanda', a song about the genocide by the punk ska band Rancid. In fairness, having since heard the original I have realised there wasn't much to murder.

Nicholas finally arrived the next morning with a beaming smile and a cast-iron handshake. He had come from Uganda in a beaten-up minibus that looked like something out of *Mad Max*. 'We made it!' he and his passenger, the faithful Simon, yelled. Without so much as stopping, they roared off with a final exhortation, 'There's no time to lose, everyone's at the Amahoro Stadium, follow me!'

And, sure enough, everyone was at the Amahoro Stadium. This national stadium, like so much recent infrastructure, had been built by the Chinese. It housed offices of all the sporting organisations, cheap rooms for competitors, and indoor and outdoor arenas.

Our welcoming committee included Dominic Biscwana from the Rwandan Paralympic Committee, Pierre Rwaka from the Rwandan Olympic Committee, Jules Ndashimye from the Rwandan Handicapped Association, and Robert Mugisha and Charles Haba from the Rwandan Cricket Association. Added to this fine group was a delegation of similarly titled dignitaries who'd driven up from Burundi, and the British ambassador's gofer. This made it, all in all, the most impressive bunch of people we'd come across in all of our travels.

They were obviously taking our visit seriously, and had also assembled a group of nervous-looking young girls and boys, 31 in total, seventeen of whom suffered from some form of blindness and fourteen with a physical disability. They were accompanied by nine blind coaches and eight with a physical disability.

While the official introductions were being made and the days were being planned, Philip told me the story of the stadium. 'Amahoro' means 'peace' in Kinyarwandan, but in 1994 it became the base for the Canadian Lt. General Romeo Dallaire's UN forces, whose job in theory was to keep the peace. However, their political masters, primarily the UN's Kofi Annan and US President Clinton, gave orders that meant Dallaire's troops had to stand by and watch as a million died. While watching they were attacked too, being midway between the airport and Kigali, and midway between the Rwandan government and the RPF forces. Dallaire's book, *Shake Hands with the Devil*, is a terrifying description of this 'failure of humanity' in Rwanda.

But now that Amahoro meant peace again, it seemed a fitting place to work, although the UN base was still there, their soldiers looking on with some concern. Our kit seemed to make them nervous – I suppose from a distance our cricket bats might have looked something like machetes, together with cricket balls which through a long lens could perhaps be construed as grenades. The stadium featured in a 2010 'good news' football movie called *Africa United*, about a group of young Rwandans trying to get to South Africa for the World Cup, but the UN's continuing presence was neatly avoided.

Nicholas had said that most of the Rwandans would understand English but that the Burundians wouldn't, having maintained their Belgian French. The ICC and the MCC produce some wonderful stuff in French describing the laws of the game, but I'd shown the material to an anglicised French chum in London, Georges, who said that whoever had written it obviously knew a lot about French, but not a lot about cricket.

Georges' family had escaped to England with General De Gaulle in 1940, but he'd been brought up as Anglo-French and sent to an English public school, where he'd been coached by Alan 'Peachy' Peach, a leg-spinning all-rounder who'd played for Surrey in the 1920s, toured the West Indies, and was famous for two (or strictly three) things: discovering the Bedser twins, and being the finest poacher in Berkshire.

So, Georges had translated the laws immaculately for me, and, for the first time, these ten pages of the laws of blind cricket were about to be unleashed on our new friends from Burundi. 'Peachy' would have been proud.

I discovered that one of the reasons the Burundians had been invited was because their country had been involved in the genocide too. The catalyst for the start of the mass murder was the mysterious shooting down of the aircraft carrying the presidents of both Rwanda and Burundi at Kigali airport only a mile or two from the Amahoro Stadium, killing both. Subsequently, Tutsis in Burundi were just as vulnerable as those in Rwanda, so the emphasis on reconciliation was all-pervasive.

Speeches were made which highlighted the new reality that in both Rwanda and Burundi the distinction between Hutu and Tutsi had been officially abolished and all were now either Rwandan or Burundian. This gathering was to celebrate that fact and to give people the chance to discover a new sport that could help link their countries to the world around them.

I'm always amazed at how young people from whatever background and with whatever disability can very quickly grasp the essence of cricket. The groups this time were perhaps the keenest we'd ever come across and were soon converted. It almost mirrors the religious conversion to Christianity that the 19th century explorers to the region such as Livingstone brought with them, but while religion has brought with it enduring problems of confrontation in Africa and elsewhere, sport has the ability to swerve most of these issues and concentrate just on the pleasure of performance, at whatever level.

To demonstrate the pleasure of cricket to the blind youngsters, Kerryn Seal had come with us again, but this time Simon Ojok was leading the sessions, so we had a Ugandan teaching Rwandans and Burundians, supervised by a Welshman, with a Jamaican, an Antiguan and a few English people looking on – truly *jeux sans frontieres*, but thankfully without the effervescent Stuart Hall.

As often happens, one boy, Jean-Marie, stood out immediately. He was smaller than the others, no more than four feet tall, and had come from Burundi. This was the first time he'd been out of his native land. Suzanne, his teacher from Burundi, told me that he was 13 years old and was almost blind. He'd come from an even poorer background than the rest of the children, and she said that his terrible diet had caused both his lack of height and the loss of his eyesight. However, he was a natural athlete, and by the end of the day was hitting the ball out of the basketball court we'd commandeered for training and into the adjacent UN compound, causing further consternation to the bemused soldiers.

We were making a small film of the work and I later interviewed Suzanne in her native French to find out what she thought of the goings on. She was a PE teacher, keen on handball, and had never seen cricket before. But she could see the pleasure it was giving to all the kids and, surprisingly, how easy it was to teach. '*C'est un jeu pour tout le monde.*' — it's a game for everybody — was her summation of cricket, which is such a nice way to describe the game and, from my own point of view as a very modest player, heartening to hear. It's given me so much pleasure over the years to be able to play with people far better than me, and to me as well it's a game for everybody.

Talking to Suzanne made me think of my wife, who is also called Suzanne and whose birthday it was the following day. It's never good to be away on birthdays. January's an awful month in England, whereas to be honest sunny Rwanda was pretty pleasant and our new friends were wonderful. My by now old friend Simon seemed to sense that something was awry, so I told him about the birthday problem. 'You must ring her tomorrow,' he said, 'and we'll all wish her happy birthday.'

And so we did. I dutifully made the call, which went down well, and then Simon grabbed the phone and said: 'Hello, Lady Suzanne, I am Simon, friend of Tom, and I am wishing you happy birthday. But now we have a surprise for you, we are all going to sing.' Simon gesticulated to all the coaches and kids to come together by the phone. They all sang together, the Rwandans with 'Happy birthday to you, happy birthday to you, happy birthday dear Lady Suzanne, happy birthday to you,' and the Burundians to the same familiar tune but with the French words '*Joyeux anniversaire*'. I don't know where the sudden elevation to the peerage came from, but Suzanne said it was the nicest surprise she'd had in years.

A few weeks later, back home in England, a parcel arrived from Simon in Uganda. In it was a letter to the newly ennobled Lady Suzanne, with a hand-carved Jomo Kenyatta-style fly whisk in the shape of a giraffe enclosed as a belated birthday present. I'm looking at it now hanging on my window, and woe betide any flies coming its way.

As I'd unwittingly created a diversion to the day, Mikey then announced to all and sundry that as a thank you to everyone for the birthday song 'the Major's going to do a bowling masterclass, to show how it's really done.' He then burst into a fit of hysterical laughter. Now as anyone who has seen me bowl will tell you, the idea of my performing a bowling masterclass is a serious oxymoron. I bowl very slowly off a surprisingly long run, the only possible danger to the batsman being the angle at which the ball comes down from a great height. They were called donkey drops in the old days, but, understandably, seem to have become largely extinct.

Of course my audience knew nothing of this, and as old age is revered in Africa the level of anticipation was palpable. Mikey announced that the best way to get a batsman out was to bowl them with a ball pitching on middle stump and hitting the top of the off stump, 'and the Major will now demonstrate this.' He asked for complete silence, not only from the assembled crowd (suddenly much bigger than it had been ten minutes earlier) but also from the UN base next door. 'To make the ball perform this magic, the Major needs to con-cen-trate. Shhh. And we don't want no batsman in the way, this is pure bowlin'.'

The fervent cry for 'Shhh' reminded me of the opening lines of Henry Newbolt's famous poem:

There's a breathless hush in the Close tonight.
Ten to make and the match to win.
A bumping pitch and a blinding light.

It's a poem about a young boy at Clifton School who grows up to fight in Africa. This wasn't Clifton School, but it was certainly Africa. Some less well-known lines from the second stanza are sadly applicable to Rwanda:

The sand of the desert is sodden red,
Red with the wreck of a square that broke ...
The river of death has brimmed his banks ...

I doubt if the Amahoro Stadium had ever witnessed such silence, or such pressure heaped onto one individual, at least in peacetime. I'd had no time to remonstrate with Mikey and there was now no backing out. I just had to give it a go. I took a slightly longer run-up than usual, and bowled slightly faster too, up to snail as opposed to the normal slug pace. The ball looped towards the wicket. It did pitch on middle, albeit a bit short. Then it hit a small bump of red clay, just as in Newbolt's poem, and jumped to the left, just enough to hit the bail on the top of the imaginary right-handed batsman's off stump.

In time-honoured fashion, the stadium erupted, and yet again I was surrounded by everyone, this time congratulating me on my bowling, which generated a new nickname, 'The Magical Major'. Amid all the whooping and hollering, one cry stood out: 'I say, old boy, well done.' It was the British ambassador, who'd crept in unbeknown to me at the back and had witnessed the entire miracle. So impressed was he with all the activity and the good vibes coming back from the local dignitaries about the work being done, he'd decided to extend the guest list for his party the following evening to include all the kids and coaches, because he wanted to have a cricket match on his lawn 'as well as lots to eat and drink'.

We finished before it got too hot, and got back to the famous swimming pool at the Milles Collines to celebrate my bowling miracle in the traditional way, with me buying all the beers.

Philip brought us back to earth, reminding us that we'd agreed to visit the genocide memorials in and around Kigali. Strange that these had now become tourist sites, a bit like Auschwitz concentration camp near Krakow, but to understand Rwanda it's important to understand its recent history, so we drank up and soon sobered up at some of the statistics Philip gave us: 1,074,017 were killed, of which 93.6 per cent were Tutsis. The others were Hutus married to Tutsis; those who resembled Tutsis; those who had hidden their Tutsi neighbours; or those who were Hutus who opposed genocide. 'And all this in a hundred days while the West looked on.'

These are the official Rwanda government figures. The population of Rwanda at the time was around seven million, so some fifteen per cent of the total had been killed. The equivalent figure in the UK would have been nine million.

The Gisozi Genocide Memorial in Kigali contains the remains of a quarter of a million of these victims. But despite this astonishing figure, there are two memorials outside Kigali which are even more affecting. At Nyamata, about 30km from Kigali, the church holds the remains of the hundreds of victims who sought refuge there but who were murdered in cold blood. Some of that blood can still be seen on the walls. In the gardens around the church, a group of men were working away, wearing what looked like pink pyjamas. Philip explained that these men were ex-members of the 'Interahamwe' or 'those who kill together' – the men who did the dirty work in 1994. In French they're called 'Genocidaires'. The work they were doing and the clothes they were wearing were designed to make everyone know who they were and why they were there.

Next to another church in nearby Nyarama are the remains of some of the 5,000 who were murdered there. Their clothes are still piled up as witness to the fact. I was walking along with head bowed when I noticed a well-worn grey aluminium one franc coin, dated 1974. It must have fallen from someone's pocket as they tried to run away. I picked it up and now I keep it on my desk to remind me of what man can do to man, and of the fact that in both cases the churches involved didn't do much to stop the suffering.

The next day was spent practising for the main event at the British embassy that was to take place late that afternoon. The media machine had been alerted, so all the kids felt like stars already, having been on radio, TV and in the press. It was very unusual for all the kids to be invited to an official reception at the grand embassy building in the best part of town, but the ambassador was a very unusual man, and determined to demonstrate that British government support for was for all the people of Rwanda, not just those at the top. A cavalcade of minibuses carried the very excited group up the hill to the diplomatic district, right next to one of the main Rwandan government buildings.

The food and drink provided for the kids was wolfed down. They'd been well looked after at the Amahoro hostel, but it's easy to forget that many of these young people spend most of their time hungry, so to be faced with a feast was quite overwhelming.

The match had to wait for the arrival of the Rwandan sports minister, who was in a meeting in the building next door. By the time he arrived, there'd been time for some practice on the lawn. It wasn't quite big enough for a full ground but was a decent area nevertheless. The sports minister insisted on umpiring, which was a problem as he had no knowledge of the laws whatsoever, although I have to say I've come across many umpires like that. So, Charles Haba from the Rwandan Cricket Association gave him a quick crash course and the game started. My bowling quickly reverted to type and I was soon replaced by Mikey, whose performance was a proper masterclass, unlike my fluke on the previous day.

We'd mixed up blind cricket with disability cricket and able-bodied cricket, so it was a bit difficult to keep up with both scores and rules, but with the tropical dusk rapidly descending we decided that there was one over left and 16 to win. Little Jean-Marie came in to bat. Over the week he'd eaten so much food that I reckon he'd grown a few inches – he looked as fit as a fiddle and full of confidence.

The discussion as to who should bowl the last over was soon taken out of our hands as the ambassador grabbed the ball. 'I know we're trying to help them, but we do want to win, you know,' he said as he marked out his run. I tried to warn him that Jean-Marie was actually rather good, but he'd already started running in. His first ball went into the bushes for four, as did his second and indeed his third. 'Think I'll take some pace off the ball, that'll fool the blighter,' he murmured. It didn't. His flighted delivery was struck for six over the trees and into the road, the ball was lost forever and the match won by Jean-Marie and his team of new cricketing all-stars.

The kids then queued up for their T-shirts and certificates and politely listened to some stirring words from the sports minister and the ambassador. Both had been amazed at what they'd seen and both were genuinely enthusiastic, not just for the sporting future of Rwanda but for the new spirit of togetherness between Hutu and Tutsi, able-bodied and disabled, which these few days had witnessed.

Jean-Marie answered for the Burundian kids with a few words about how much he'd enjoyed the cricket and, more importantly, the food. Nicholas watched and quietly applauded with a satisfied smile on his face. He mouthed across to me 'See you in Tanzania', as he slipped away into the night.

With a day off before our flight home, Philip had insisted that we see one of the other great sights of Rwanda — the mountain gorillas of the Virunga National Park. The park straddles the border with the Democratic Republic of Congo (DRC) and is a couple of hours' easy drive north-west from Kigali along a fine new road built by the ever-present Chinese.

I sat next to Philip in the minibus. Now was the time to hear his story.

His schooling had gone well in Kampala, and from there he graduated to Makerere University, the same place Simon would graduate from a few years hence. In Uganda, he was forced to join Laurent Kabila's Rwandan National Front (RPF), who were planning a guerrilla campaign against the ruling Hutu government in Rwanda. He wanted to continue his studies, but the RPF insisted on his joining them because he was fit, young and clever. They said that not joining the RPF could endanger his safety, which soon made his mind up. I expected the RPF to be a classic bunch of committed 'insurgents', but Philip insisted that this was not the case, certainly not in the beginning.

In 1990 Kabila's RPF forces, including Philip, crossed the border into Rwanda and started their anti-government campaign. Like most guerrilla wars, it was messy and stop-start, with as many failures as successes. Gradually, however, the impetus increased — the force became more professional and better equipped as support came in from Uganda and elsewhere.

By 1994 a full-scale war was being fought. As the RPF approached Kabila, including their 'mistaken' shelling of the UN compound at Amahoro, the full reality of the genocide became apparent. What was left of the Hutu government and its forces fled to the Democratic Republic of Congo.

The RPF took over in Rwanda and eventually Kabila was installed as the new president, with a mandate, despite his Tutsi heritage, to unite the country as one.

Philip said it was hard to adjust to normal life after four years of guerrilla warfare, but he tried to, and became a tour guide and fixer for the increasing numbers of aid workers and tourists who wanted to visit Rwanda. In the four years of fighting he hadn't heard anything of his mother and father, who had paid for his education in Uganda, or of his brother and sister.

He went back to the family home and discovered that they had all been murdered. He was determined to find out who was responsible, and local survivors told him that it was the young man who had lived next door, a Hutu the same age as Philip. He had been his best friend at school.

Then began a seven-year hunt for the murderer. Had he survived and if so where was he? It took seven years because hundreds of thousands of people in a similar situation to Philip were trying to do the same, and almost the entire civil service had either been wiped out or fled to the DRC, so records were sparse. He finally tracked the suspect down to a prison in Kigali and confronted him with the question he'd been wanting to ask for so long: 'Did you kill my mother, my father, my sister and my brother?' He said there was a long silence before the answer came: 'Yes.' With that answer, Philip got up and left the prison cell.

Nothing could bring back his family, and he'd found their murderer, who had been punished. Philip had witnessed so much death in the war that he didn't wish for any more violence. He said that his old school friend would spend the rest of his life in jail, which, now that he had been confronted by his past, was worse than being dead.

The Virunga National Park was founded in 1925 – it was the first in Africa – and straddles the remains of eight volcanoes, which rise as high as 4,500ft. Its coolness, rainfall and vegetation make it the perfect habitat for the mountain gorilla, one of the world's most endangered species. Only about 300 are left, half in the DRC, where they are prey to poachers looking for bush meat, and half in Rwanda, where well-trained and well-armed park rangers guide small parties of tourists to see them in the wild. The large fee charged (about $375) helps pay for the gorillas' survival in one of the world's flashpoints. Diane Fossey devoted most of her short life to the preservation of these magnificent beasts and her story was told in *Gorillas in the Mist*. She was murdered in 1985 for her work, and now the gorillas she hoped to protect were in the midst of the DRC's civil war.

There are so few gorillas left that all are known by name, and our guide told us that if we were lucky we should be able to encounter the Sabyinyo group who live between Mounts Sabyinyo and Gahinga. They are led by the most famous silverback gorilla in the Virungas, Guhondo, who at 220kg is the heaviest gorilla on record. Because of this I was a little nervous about personally meeting Guhondo, despite the fact that *Bradt's Guide* says that 'the gorilla is an ape of formidable size but peaceful temperament'.

This peaceful temperament is obviously not of much help when you've chosen to live in one of the most dangerous places on earth. As we climbed up to the peak of Mount Sabyinyo, we could see the lights of Goma in the distance through the mist, and hear gunfire – ample evidence as to why this provincial town in the DRC has a reputation of which Dodge City would have been proud.

Suddenly our guide said, 'Freeze, they are close by.' Sure enough, a few minutes later, there was a massive rustling behind me and Guhondo rushed past, followed by three much smaller gorillas, brushing the sleeve of my coat. He was huge, about seven feet tall and four feet across. I just hoped he was in a good mood. He stopped and looked back, and gave me an old-fashioned look before speeding on for his lunch. David Attenborough has said, 'There is more meaning and mutual understanding in exchanging a glance with a gorilla than any other animal I know.' How right he is.

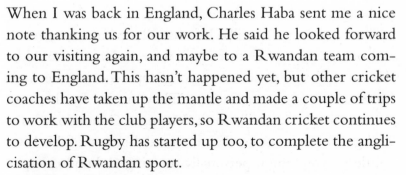

When I was back in England, Charles Haba sent me a nice note thanking us for our work. He said he looked forward to our visiting again, and maybe to a Rwandan team coming to England. This hasn't happened yet, but other cricket coaches have taken up the mantle and made a couple of trips to work with the club players, so Rwandan cricket continues to develop. Rugby has started up too, to complete the anglicisation of Rwandan sport.

On the political front, at the Commonwealth Conference in 2007 Rwanda was proposed for full membership, with

Tony Blair apparently backing the motion with the words 'Well, they do play cricket don't they?' In November 2009 Rwanda did indeed became a full member of the British Commonwealth. At this historic news, Charles Haba was quoted as saying: 'I think you can say we have batted our way into the Commonwealth.' So, as the old saying goes, cricket was the winner in Rwanda.

13

TANZANIA – WHATEVER HAPPENED TO TANGANYIKA?

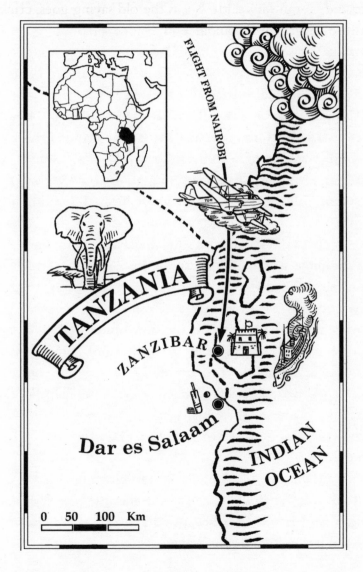

HARRY CAMPBELL WROTE a surprisingly funny book called *Whatever Happened to Tanganyika?* in which he listed all the great names lost to geography. Tanganyika became British after the First World War and remained so until independence in December 1963. A month later, in January 1964, it invaded the neighbouring island of Zanzibar – also recently independent – to create Tanzania. This made poor little Zanzibar the only country in the world never to have taken its seat at the United Nations. Now there's a pub quiz answer for you.

Although, like many African countries it had a bloodthirsty start to its life, Tanzania has largely avoided the kind of conflict witnessed in its neighbours, Uganda, Rwanda and Burundi. That might have been something to do with its first president, Julius Nyerere, who was educated at Edinburgh University. Despite sporting a Hitler moustache, he seems to have been a mild-mannered sort of a chap, having translated the complete works of Shakespeare into Swahili, and having been an aficionado both of book binding, and of sipping that stalwart of 1970s dinner parties, Mateus Rose.

However, peace was suddenly interrupted in 1998, when a fellow most of us had never really heard of before, Osama bin Laden, organised the bombing of the US embassy in Dar es Salaam, which killed eleven people. Another bomb in Nairobi killed many more, but we in the West didn't take much notice of it. Hmm. Only three years later came 9/11.

Despite this, the third and, as it transpired, final leg of our East African Disability Cricket Programme was less traumatic than the first two, because the people themselves had suffered less trauma in recent years.

The trip had been hanging in the balance for some time, as funding was in short supply. As often happens, early enthusiasm for projects dies away over time as the original protagonists move on. However, we didn't want to let Nicholas Muramagi down, so we tried everyone we could to enable the programme to keep going. Eventually the final funding jigsaw piece came from an unlikely source.

God knows why, but I'd had a sudden naive inspiration (since thankfully lost) to become a proper umpire. It was probably just because I wanted to understand exactly why I kept being given out LBW. My deluded rationale was that it clearly had nothing to do with my lack of talent, and that therefore it must be The Laws of Cricket that were at fault. So, I attended an umpires' introduction course at Dulwich Cricket Club. It just so happened that at the time their affable president, one John Smith, was holding forth at the bar, not greatly interested in the umpires' course.

I'd spent many a day with him at Lord's and he asked what my plans were for the winter. I explained the boring funding problems we were having getting the Tanzania leg off the ground, and he immediately said in his magisterial Middlesburian way, 'I'm sure Hazel will sort you out, here are her details.' Hazel is his wife, but is also the daughter of perhaps the most famous English lady cricketer, Rachael Heyhoe Flint, and has inherited her mother's passion for the game. At the time she was working for Kenya Airways. After only a couple of meetings with her, in exchange for an article in their in-flight magazine about our trip, we were landing in Nairobi, on our way to Zanzibar from where we would head on to our final destination on the mainland, Dar es Salaam.

Zanzibar was a side trip, but everyone said that if we were going all the way to Tanzania we must go there. All the great explorers passed through Zanzibar, and as we grandly regarded ourselves as such, it seemed churlish not to. The explorer Richard Burton said on his first sight of 'the mysterious island' in 1857 that 'earth, sea and sky all seemed wrapped in a soft and sensuous repose', although these sound like the sort of words that could equally have come from the other Richard Burton, the great actor who married Elizabeth Taylor. Twice. Our old friend Speke, after whom our hotel in Kampala, Uganda, had been named, travelled there with the first Richard Burton, followed by Livingstone, who arrived in 1866. Stanley, his discoverer came in 1872, before Livingstone departed in a coffin in 1874. That's an awful lot of explorers.

We weren't visiting Zanzibar for the cricket, but an old guidebook from the 1960s mentioned cricket being played there, and on the road from the airport to Stone Town one could see the obvious remains of a derelict ground and pavilion. Actually, we soon discovered that cricket hadn't been played in Zanzibar for many years, until an intrepid team of cricketing explorers, the MCC, had played (and naturally won) a game there only the previous month, before travelling on, like us, to Dar es Salaam.

This was a bit like Scott finding that Amundsen had reached the South Pole just before him in 1912, although Amundsen had had the good manners to send a telegram to Scott in 1910 warning him: 'Beg leave inform you proceeding Antarctic. Amundsen.' We'd had nothing from the MCC, but, like Scott, we ploughed on regardless and, unlike poor Scott, survived.

Zanzibar was always famous for its spices and cloves, but now tourists pile in to see where Freddie Mercury, born Farok Bulsara to Parsee parents in 1946, started his life in the old Residency Road right in the middle of Stone Town.

But sadly it was slavery which made Zanzibar, and which first attracted Livingstone to the island, and indeed to Africa. The slave trade was run by the Omanis, and it's estimated that over a million left Zanzibar for slavery before the practice was finally abolished, surprisingly late, in 1917. The Anglican Cathedral was built on the site of the old slave market, but Mikey wanted to see the slave chambers that still existed next to it. Here, up to 75 slaves were held in each dingy, windowless cell until market day. Mikey's huge frame only just fitted through into one of these cells. Having squeezed himself in he immediately wanted to get out, because he could sense the presence of evil spirits in the dark, damp chambers.

The journey across the Zanzibar Channel is only about 50 miles and we took the ferry *MV Spice Islander*, which was not as exotic as it sounds. The ship was terribly overcrowded, and struggled across the benign sea. Dar es Salaam is Arabic for 'safe port' and thankfully we arrived safely, looking forward to seeing our friends Nicholas and Simon again. Some time later, however, I read that the good ship *MV Spice Islander* had capsized and sunk between Dar es Salaam and

Zanzibar, with over 200 feared drowned. It had been carrying over 800 passengers instead of its legal limit of 600, and was overloaded with building materials and plant equipment.

Like most of the cities in sub-Saharan Africa, Dar es Salaam is full of fading monuments to the optimism of the 1960s era of independence, although there are still some traces of the turn of the 20th century German colonial era, such as a railway station which wouldn't look out of place in Bavaria.

Because German and British East Africa were next to each other, one of the more bizarre campaigns of the First World War took place in the region, for the entire duration of the conflict. Try as they might, British African forces could not defeat the German African forces led by the wonderfully named Lieutenant Colonel (later Generalmajor) Paul Emil von Lettow-Vorbeck, who rampaged across British, German and Portuguese East Africa, before finally surrendering, undefeated, in Abercorn (now Mbala in what was Northern Rhodesia), 12 days after the European armistice.

Giles Foden has written about this war in *Mimi and Tutou Go Forth,* as has William Boyd in his *An Ice Cream War,* so-called because one of the British soldiers said at the time: 'We will all melt like ice cream in the sun.' Judging by the result it seems like they did.

The MCC team touring Tanzania just before us took a leaf out of von Lettow-Vorbeck's book by also being undefeated in all their matches, but found the cricket much harder than they'd expected.

The main ground in Dar es Salaam is at the Mlimani campus of the University of Dar es Salaam, another series of 1960s monuments to optimism sprawled across a hill overlooking the city. Although the site is undeniably tropical and

African, the buildings could have been a part of any English university built in the 1960s, such as Sussex or East Anglia.

The students looked just the same as English students, too, either rushing late to lectures overburdened with books, or lounging around under trees. Also like its counterparts in England, the university has a strong radical heritage, having educated three African presidents – the president of Tanzania, the president of the Democratic Republic of the Congo, and my old friend Nagenda's boss in Uganda, President Museveni.

At the foot of the hill was the ground, a beautifully manicured stretch of land with a cricket pavilion that would have graced any English village club. There is something wonderfully homely and comforting about cricket pavilions, wherever they are – the benches outside, the obligatory tea urn and the faded notices inside give them a unique atmosphere. Tim Rice's brother Jonathan wrote a lovely book called *The Pavilion Book of Pavilions*, which always cheers me up if I'm suffering from mid-winter blues. We held the wake for my mother in the pavilion at Grace Road, Leicester, and I celebrated that sad day by having a bench placed outside the pavilion in memory of both my mother and father. When watching cricket there, I've even asked people sitting on it to move because it's 'my' bench, my *lebensraum* – very uncharitable of me, but I hope understandable.

Our welcoming committee was almost as impressive as in Rwanda, with Iddi Kibwana from the Sports Association for the Disabled, Rish Urio from the Ministry of Sports and Eliwaja Jacob, a teacher specialising in the visually impaired from Morogoro Teachers College, which is based about a hundred miles west of Dar es Salaam. Eliwaja had brought with her a busload of her pupils, all hugely excited not only to have the chance to learn about a new sport but also to visit Dar es Salaam, most of them for the first time. Iddi and Rish had brought a group of local kids to the ground, and they immediately started chattering to the out-of-towners, comparing notes about teachers and mates, just like all kids do.

But, as in Rwanda, there was no sign of Nicholas or Simon yet. They were driving down, and it's an awfully long way from Kampala – all the way round Lake Victoria and then across the entire width of a very large and dusty country. So we started without them, but were immediately helped by a group of young local players, all very smartly kitted out, who were practising on the outfield. It turned out that this was the Tanzanian national team, all of whom had played against the MCC the previous month and were keenly honing new skills learnt from the opposition.

The captain was Hamis Abdallah, a tall and rangy bowl- ing all-rounder who said that the MCC visit had been the highlight of his cricketing life, and that he couldn't wait to get to England to play – something which the ICC had promised as part of their build-up to their World Cup quali- fying games. Geoff Smith and the blind cricket coaches demonstrated the game to Hamis, and after his astonishment had subsided he joined in with helping the kids get to know the game.

Then 'Mad Max' Nicholas Muramagi hove into view, a cloud of dust billowing behind his minibus as if he'd been competing in the East African bus rally. He really had, as it had taken them 30 hours of hard driving to get to us, though luckily they'd broken down only once. Even behind the dust-covered windscreen we could see their enormous smiles at having finally made it.

The Dar es Salaam *Daily News* heralded our visit with a nice article entitled 'Blind Cricket to be Developed', which tells it like it is. But we were overshadowed by a football story — 'Hapless Simba held by Ashanti', which had a bit more oomph to it. The relatively peaceful nature of Tanzania compared to its neighbours was emphasised by other stories in the newspaper, one of which caught my eye — I just had to read on when I saw the headline 'Dar resident jailed five years for stealing a goat worth 65,000/—'.

This seemed a bit harsh. The poor chap did try to explain the situation, stating that he entered the goat's enclosure while naked and asking for leniency as his intention had not been to steal the goat but to have a romantic evening with it. Could have happened to anyone really — obviously just a situation that got a bit out of hand. Still, in his five-year stretch he'll at least have plenty of time to think about the goat. It's a bit like the jokes about the Welsh and sheep, which of course have no basis in fact whatsoever.

The presence of the Tanzanian team made the cricket even more interesting than usual. Mikey was able to help the kids out with some serious one-to-one work, and the team joined in helping Geoff coach the blind kids. Although most of Mikey's recent cricket coaching has been in the disability and inner-city environments, he remains an excellent coach of talented mainstream cricketers as well. As so often happens, players who never quite made it often make the best coaches because they know how hard the game is at the top level. The same is true of most sports. Neither Sir Alex Ferguson nor Arsène Wenger set the world alight as footballers, but they are arguably the top two football coaches of their generation.

Eliwaja had never seen sport used to help her blind pupils before and was amazed at the progress they made in their few days of playing and being coached. Most of all, she said it gave them new confidence in themselves and in their abilities. She wished all of her pupils could have come, and vowed to take the game back to Morogoro and spread the word. She spent a lot of time talking to Nicholas, Simon, Iddi and Rish about how they were going to develop the game across the region and, because of the involvement of the Tanzanian players, how it could be integrated with the Tanzania Cricket Association. In a country where cricket has to battle for its very existence, this sort of collaboration is essential: everyone has to work together.

For our final night in Tanzania, we all went out to the Mashua bar on the Msasani slipway, a place where both ex-pats and the wealthier locals hang out. The music was Western as well as African, making everyone happy. There was even an African karaoke, which Nicholas enjoyed, but the highlight of the evening was undoubtedly Mikey's 'Slavery Rap'.

The visit to the slave cells in Stone Town in Zanzibar had affected him, and he'd been thinking about putting his feelings to music. The locals didn't know what to expect when he began to head for the stage, with me leading him on through the crowd as his bodyguard – a reversal of the racial stereotype. Mikey's very presence hushed the audience, who were at first mystified by his rap, particularly its serious content. Within minutes, however, all joined in, black, white and brown, to celebrate with Mikey the freedom of the black man and the end of slavery, which Livingstone had first sought some 150 years previously.

Our farewell to Nicholas and Simon was an emotional one because although we'd successfully completed the third leg of our East African odyssey, the fourth was in jeopardy because tribal tensions were rising in Kenya in advance of elections. Nicholas said he had something for me. It was a present to remember him by. It was a large envelope containing a drawing of me, which he'd had done in the market in Dar es Salaam, taken from a photograph I'd given him in Rwanda. It wasn't a bad likeness, and above the drawing were the words 'Experienced Global Man', which I rather like – a homage to age and to travel from a man who'd become a dear friend.

It was astonishing what Nicholas had achieved, and it was easy to forget that we'd only met two years previously in Zambia because he couldn't afford the departure tax at Livingstone airport. Europeans write off Africa at their peril, as we were soon to find out in Sierra Leone, another country benighted by civil war but determined to rise again, peacefully.

Sadly that message had yet to penetrate Kenya, whose tribal problems were soon to be compounded by wars on its northern and eastern frontiers in Sudan and Somalia. This meant we were prevented from bringing our versions of the game to arguably the most developed cricketing nation in East Africa. Sierra Leone, on the other side of the continent would be a very different challenge.

On 14 February 2008, four months after our return to England, a Valentine's Day email pinged into my inbox. It was from Eliwaja Jacob, the teacher from Morogoro. She said that earlier that day she'd received one from Simon and she hoped my wife wouldn't mind my receiving one from her. She said that her blind kids were doing really well, loving both playing cricket and introducing it to all the kids at the college. She said that 'disability is not inability' and that cricket had helped her kids believe that. I thought of my father, born on Valentine's Day 1899, who had first introduced me to cricket. And I'd been able to pass on my love of the game, on the day of love, to a wonderful teacher in Tanzania.

Later that year, in August, I saw in my local paper that a team from Tanzania was playing that weekend at Amersham, the club where I'd first introduced cricket to my son about fifteen years previously. It's a lovely ground overlooked by Shardelows House, so I went along for old times' sake, even though I hadn't heard from any of the Tanzanian players since my return.

Amersham were batting and doing reasonably well. I thought I recognised the bowler coming in at a fair pace from the pavilion end. At the end of the over, he walked down towards me on the boundary to take up his position at third man. Third Man in Amersham. A smile of Nicholas Muramagi proportions spread across his face. It was Hamis Abdallah, on tour with the Tanzania team, just as the ICC had promised. The game stopped as the other players such as Benson and Rashidi, who I'd also met in Dar es Salaam, rushed across to greet me. I ushered them back to the match, because you know what umpires can be like, but afterwards in the bar I introduced them to Fuller's London Pride, just as they'd introduced me to Premium Serengeti Lager back in far off Dar es Salaam.

Contacts were made during this tour which meant that, encouraged by the ICC, the team came again in 2010 to play in Hertfordshire. And now two Tanzanian players come across every year to play good quality club cricket with Watford CC in the Hertfordshire league, so that they can improve their game and take back their knowledge to Tanzania. Keep a look out for them — they're going to be good.

14

SIERRA LEONE – LAND OF IRON AND DIAMONDS

W**E'D BEEN WARNED** that the best way to get through the long customs queues at the grandly named Inter City Air Terminal at Freetown's Lungi International Airport was to bribe your way through, so in no time we were being welcomed into the steamy Sierra Leone night by Sidney Benka-Coker, the secretary of the Sierra Leone Cricket Association. Sidney was a tall, studious-looking older man with the bearing of an athlete, and maybe a touch of Clive Lloyd about him. I think he'd like this description, as his eyes lit up behind his horn-rimmed glasses at the bags of cricket kit we'd brought for him. He said that he came from a long line of cricket enthusiasts and proudly announced that he had two cousins called Ponsford and Bradman, so his Sidney probably referred to Sidney Barnes. I later discovered that in fact his full title was General Sidney Benka-Coker, so he was definitely not a man to mess with.

But before we could discuss cricket any more, we first had to decide how to get to our hotel at Lumley Beach on the western edge of Freetown. Lungi International Airport is extraordinarily inappropriately situated for access to Freetown, a bit like those airports used by cheap airlines that turn out to be miles from their stated destination. It's the other side of the wide mouth of the Sierra Leone River, which forms Freetown's harbour, the third biggest in the world.

Sidney explained that there were four options. The most popular route was the old ferry, which was cheap but took three hours and was normally dangerously overcrowded. It was also possible to go by taxi, but this meant a five-hour 90-mile journey inland to Port Loco before heading back south-west to Freetown on roads which were virtually impassable and prone to attack from armed robbers. Then there was the ex-English Channel hovercraft, which was quick, more expensive, but often broke down in mid-estuary with no mechanic on board and only the aforementioned ferry to tow it back. The final option was a 30-year-old Russian Mil Mi-8 helicopter, which looked like a giant, prehistoric monster. This was the quickest and most expensive, but its sister aircraft had crashed while trying to land at Lungi the previous year, killing 22 officials from the Togo Football Association, including their sports minister.

I went out onto the tarmac to inspect the helicopter. It looked a bit rusty, but the engine was running, the blades were idly turning, and the pilot gave me a cheery thumbs up. To clinch the decision, Sidney said that our local fixer, David Turner, was waiting for us at Paddy's Bar, close to Lumley and the heliport, so we paid our fares and clambered aboard. I'd never been in a helicopter before and am not keen to repeat the experience, at least not in a 30-year-old Mil Mi-8, but, still shaking from the noisy, shuddering journey, we landed at the Mammy Yoko (*sic*) Heliport, Freetown.

I was happy to be back in Graham Greene territory, for he arrived in Freetown in 1935 aboard the aptly named *SS David Livingstone* with his cousin Barbara. He was there to write *Journey without Maps*, a travel book describing his journey across Sierra Leone and neighbouring Liberia. He wasn't keen on Sierra Leone and wrote, 'Everything ugly in Freetown was European, the stores, the churches, the government offices, the two hotels. If there was anything beautiful in the place it was native.' Later, after service in Sierra Leone during the war, he wrote *The Heart of the Matter*, set in an unnamed African country (probably Sierra Leone), which he described as 'a fly blown West African colony'.

He obviously hadn't been to Paddy's Bar, which was a typically jolly open-air African bar selling the local Star beer at bargain prices. These was great music, including the local Palm Wine music, a bizarre mixture of African rhythms and country and western, which suited both the ex-pats and locals alike. There were also the obligatory beautiful African girls looking for business.

It was good to see David again. He was a cricket fan and a 'charity professional' who'd read about our work in Rwanda and suggested, when we met in London, that we go to Sierra Leone, where he was currently working, to run a similar programme. 'Charity professional' can cover a multitude of sins, and travelling across Africa one comes across a lot of people who are more interested in themselves and in their own agendas than in really doing good. But David, with the air of a 1960s throwback despite his early middle age, had spent his life trying to do good in some of the world's worst trouble spots, and was as excited as we were at the prospect of linking up with local organisations, both charity and cricket, to try to address some of Sierra Leone's problems.

And my, what problems. In 2002, at the end of an eleven-year civil war Sierra Leone was officially the poorest country in the world. The war had been caused by the Revolutionary United Front (RUF) seeking to control the supply of what became known as 'blood diamonds'. Prior to the war, the country had been rich. I've got a set of beautiful stamps from the 1960s extolling Sierra Leone as 'The Land of Iron and Diamonds', and it seems ironic that it was those diamonds, which wedding rings have made the ultimate symbol of love, that should lead to a war which saw 50,000 die, hundreds of thousands become disabled and a million displaced. It is said that 90 per cent of the population of Sierra Leone has never even seen a diamond, yet it was diamonds that destroyed the country.

Leonardo di Caprio starred in the Hollywood movie *Blood Diamond*, which is set in Sierra Leone. It is a surprisingly good depiction of the war and of the land. Another movie, *Johnny Mad Dog*, gives an even more brutal yet brilliant portrayal of the conflict, and the scenes in the locally produced documentary *Cry Freetown* are the most upsetting I've ever seen on film, anywhere. This last film contains the chilling line: 'Sierra Leone is a country that was left to die.'

But Sierra Leone was being rebuilt, and we were there to be part of that rebuilding. Arrival at the hotel brought some light relief from David's initial briefing – it was called the Barmoi Hotel, so naturally we all became part of the 'Barmoi Army'. Oh dear, but you can't be serious all the time. The hotel was Sierra Leone's best, which is to say that it was better than the other one. Apparently David Beckham had recently stayed there on one of his charity visits, so if it was good enough for him, it was certainly good enough for us.

There was to be a lot of briefing, I guess because of the precarious state of a country trying, as it was, to reinvent itself. The British Army, as opposed to the Barmoi Army, had briefed us in London about its role in rebuilding Sierra Leone. It had been involved in ending the civil war, although the mainly Nigerian African forces, who, we were told, 'love a good fight', took the brunt of the action. This marvellously un-PC briefing on 'Human Rights in Sierra Leone' was conducted by Warrant Officer Chels Lovatt, who'd become a good friend while we'd been working with him in London to introduce the army as a possible career for some of the kids we came across in the inner city. He had suggested we hook up with his colleagues still in Sierra Leone, perhaps to help out with the coaching but mainly because, 'there's English beer at their base'. Note to diary ...

Sidney Benka-Coker briefed us about the cricket scene. He was surprised we didn't know that there had been good cricket in the region for many years, with the four West African ex-British colonies – Sierra Leone, Nigeria, Gambia and Ghana – playing regularly in a quadrangular tournament. Amazingly they had recently been joined by the ex-French colony Senegal. I then did remember that I'd read a book by J. L. Carr (whose *Dictionary of Extraordinary Cricketers* would join me with my Desert Island Discs, if I'm ever asked) called *A Season in Sinji*, set in the Gambia during the Second World War, where most of the action revolved around cricket, not war.

Sidney said that most of the Sierra Leone 1st XI and the Under-19s were either teachers or students and were qualified coaches who were keen to help us. They also wanted to show us how good they were by challenging us to a game of 'proper cricket' at the end of the week, adding pressure to an already daunting schedule.

The next thing we had to do was pay a courtesy visit to the British High Commission to get their views on the situation. These turned out to be, basically, 'It's jolly good, actually.' They seemed far keener to discuss the proposed cricket match. They'd already heard about it, and were keen to play on our side. So, some good news at last.

I wondered if one of the reasons that Graham Greene didn't much like Sierra Leone was that there was too much cricket there, but this is something we'll never know. I'd brought Greene's *Journey without Maps* with me, though, unlike Greene, I *had* been able to find a map. However, because so few visitors now go to Sierra Leone, there's no guidebook available, so for me it was to be *Journey without Guidebooks*.

The main part of our work was to introduce tapeball cricket to both able-bodied and disabled kids centred at the Conforti Community Aid Children's Organisation at Calaba Town on the eastern outskirts of Freetown. This meant a drive from the very west of Freetown to the very east, perhaps only five miles as the crow flies, but the crow doesn't fly there, and the chaotic traffic meant that it was an hour's journey right through town. Dilapidated remnants of the old colonial town still remain in the centre, but the main feature is a massive old cotton wood tree under which Freetown was founded in 1792. This tree is so important to Sierra Leone that it's even on the 20 leone banknote.

The Kroo Town Road from Lumley to Freetown passes over a creek that empties into Kroo Bay, and there we saw the worst poverty out of all the African countries we'd visited. There were acre after acre of shacks, built from anything the locals could find – old car tyres, driftwood and plastic sacks – an horrific site emphasised by the name of the road off Kroo Town Road to the creek – Grand Cess Street. Greene doesn't describe such poverty, indeed he almost suggests the opposite, so one suspects that this dereliction is a result of the 11-year civil war.

Although Sierra Leone had been the departure point for hundreds of thousands of slaves in the 17th and 18th centuries under Spanish and Portuguese rule, Freetown, as the name suggests, was later founded by the British as a home for slaves freed from other parts of the British Empire, such as Canada and the West Indies. Its Utopian dream had obviously been shattered by war.

But on arrival at Calaba Town, it was immediately obvious that Francis Mason's Conforti organisation was at least trying to rebuild that dream. There we found his office, a disability centre, two schools and a busy workshop, all surrounding a huge dusty red earth quadrangle which Francis proudly announced would be our pitch.

Francis was another tall man who was a Creole and a Catholic, a descendant of the freed slaves who, although very much the minority in Sierra Leone, are in effect the ruling class. But Francis ruled his part of Sierra Leone in a wonderfully quiet, thoughtful way, which made his achievement all the more impressive.

Calaba Town had played a key role in the civil war, as it was the gateway to Freetown, with the main road, Kissy Road, being the only route in and out. Most of the fighting in the early years of the war had taken place in the country areas. The RUF only very gradually closed in on Freetown from the Liberian border, gathering an army of captured, brainwashed and often drugged child soldiers as they took village after village with astonishing brutality. The 1996 election featured the slogan 'The future is in your hands'. To disrupt it the RUF chopped off the hands of those who were against them so that these maimed people couldn't vote, often using the child soldiers to do this horrific work.

By January 1999 the RUF had reached the outskirts of Freetown, and there they announced their chilling objective

− 'Operation annihilate every living thing'. Most of the ramshackle houses in Calaba Town, around 900 of them, were burnt to the ground, and the entire population − those who weren't killed − fled to the relative safety of west Freetown, close to the Atlantic coast at Lumley. This was where the mainly African peacekeeping force had been forced to hole up as a last stand against the rebels. *For di People*, a local newspaper, at the time summed up the situation under the banner headline: 'Rebel terror continues unabated. Nightmare at Calaba Town.'

Francis explained all this to us in a quiet matter-of-fact sort of way, which only added further impact to hearing about what had been a horrific time for the entire population of Sierra Leone. He said we must understand the history of the country because this would explain the attitude of some of the kids at the centre, many of whom were still traumatised and liable to fight among themselves over the smallest issue.

It was with a sharp intake of breath that we ventured out into the quad to meet the coaches and the kids. Normally this entails a few small groups, but our entrance coincided with breaktime, so suddenly we were engulfed by hundreds of beautifully uniformed kids, clamouring for attention and all wanting to find out about this strange game involving plastic bats, stumps and balls covered in tape.

Mikey was the centre of attraction, being the tallest and biggest. In our few days in Calaba Town he became a Pied Piper figure, surrounded by kids chanting 'Mikey, Mikey, Mikey' wherever he went. To be honest after Francis's heartbreaking briefing this was a surprise, but the resilience of the ordinary African is something we'd come to expect, and on that day joy was unconfined in Calaba, a place where only a few years previously the opposite had been true.

We were really there to help the disabled kids, who were initially in danger of being overwhelmed by the more able-bodied. Francis soon took charge, though, while most of the kids went back to their classrooms. The disabled kids were a fair bit older, and talked in a very sanguine way about what it was like to be disabled in a very poor country. One said that they'd tried to play football but able-bodied kids had run off with the ball, and they couldn't run after them. Another said that he had 'been discarded by his family members', almost as if he was being treated as litter. This was why he and all his disabled colleagues were living in dormitories at the Conforti site, all part of the total care programme organised by Francis.

There were so many kids involved that we organised half a dozen little matches at the same time on the big quad – a wonderful sight, a bit like in India on the maidans, where every inch is occupied by an impromptu game of cricket.

Having local coaches who knew about cricket was a fantastic bonus, and they immediately took over a lot of the matches. They were soon able to get the essence of the game across to young people who not only had not played cricket before, but who hadn't played any sport before. This was truly a case of taking sport to the people, rather than people to the sport, a blindingly obvious benefit in a country with few sporting facilities, but just as relevant in the UK too, where mobility and transport costs are an equally big issue. Francis summed it all up succinctly by saying, 'Sport is a powerful tool that we can use to transform the situation,' and judging by the results of just one day's work he was right.

David had organised for us to visit the British troops at their base close to the top of Leicester Peak, which overlooks Freetown, as the following day some of them were due to help out with the coaching. He said the best way was the 'pretty route' over the mountain by the Tacugama Chimpanzee Sanctuary, but he was having real difficulty persuading our driver to go that way, despite the fact that it avoided the suffocating traffic on the main road. Eventually, having been given some spare leones, he agreed. Chatting to him on the way up, I found out the reason for his reluctance. Apparently, a year or so previously a group of chimpanzees, led by the alpha male Bruno, had escaped from the sanctuary and killed a local man, as well as seriously injuring four others. And I thought chimps were jolly creatures who like their tea! Despite searching for some months, and issuing posters with a photofit picture of Bruno (actually looking pretty mild-mannered, holding a banana in his cupped hand) the Sierra Leonean police had failed to find either him or any of his mates — he was still at large, hence our driver's concern.

He drove as fast as he could along the rough mountain road. The army base was called, appropriately enough, Leicester Square. As a son of Leicester, I wondered who could have named the peak 'Leicester' and why, but my reverie was broken by the sergeant major on guard who shouted, 'Colonel Blackman's waiting for you in the bar.' My old mate Chels had lied about there being English beer there, but there was Guinness, brewed in Nigeria, as well as the local Star beer. We enjoyed a couple of hours discussing the British Army's role in Sierra Leone, which to be honest, didn't strike me as too exacting, something the colonel almost admitted, saying that it was a lot more popular a posting than Iraq or Afghanistan.

But for me the wonderful news came when he asked, 'Have you been to the Cline Town Railway Museum yet?' Not having a guidebook, I obviously hadn't. He said it was marvellous and contained a dozen or so old locos and carriages which had been found and rebuilt by army engineers with some time on their hands. Apparently, there used to be a railway going all the way up to the peak, and Greene writes about a railway journey from Freetown almost to the Liberian border at Pendembu. Cars and the war had done for these railways. However, just like in England where cars and Beeching closed so many of our railways, Sierra Leone could do with them back. As it happens, I did manage to sneak away to the museum before we left and can only report that although I was the first visitor that year, it was magical.

The following day at Calaba was magical in a different way. Everyone was on parade again, Mikey was feted as he arrived, and the army boys turned up to help. So too did the president of the Sierra Leone Cricket Association, Beresford Bournes-Coker, no doubt checking on his players, who were also helping out. In no time, the quad was full of games, which astonished Beresford, as big a cricket fan as Sidney, although not nearly as tall. Must have been a keeper, I thought, although one never wants to ask in case one gets accused of heightism.

During a break for lunch — which had been prepared and cooked in a massive iron pot by Francis's mother — one of the coaches, Ernest Mannah, came across to chat. He'd been filming as well as coaching and wanted to become a TV producer. This was interesting enough, but he then told me the story of his experiences in the civil war. A few books have been written about the war, perhaps the best known being one called *A Long Way Gone, Memoirs of a Boy Soldier*, by Ishmael Beah, but Ernest said his story was even more dramatic, and that he'd love for it to be made into a movie.

Ernest was nine years old when the RUF came through his village, killed his parents and took him away to become a child soldier. He managed to escape but was soon recaptured and punished. He said it wasn't that difficult to escape because most of the rebels were either drugged up, drunk or both. He also said that recapture was almost inevitable because the RUF had all the food, so hunger soon set in. He escaped again and was punished again, although he wasn't mutilated because he was more useful to them able-bodied. When he escaped a third time, however, his captors' patience ran out — when he was recaptured he was sentenced to death by firing squad. He was led to a clearing in the forest where the firing squad had been assembled. But just as they were about to fire someone shouted 'Stop!' The colonel in charge had recognised him. The colonel was his uncle. So Ernest was spared, but he had to fight on throughout the rest of the war until 2002 when it finally ended.

It's really hard to concentrate on anything else when one's heard such a story, so I wandered over to the workshop with Mikey for a change of scenery and to rearrange my thoughts. There, all the workers were disabled, but all were being taught new skills. Some were on sewing machines making and mending clothes. Those who could were breaking up old cars, while another group were melting down the old parts, adding in discarded drinks cans and making cooking pots like the one Francis's mother was using. Mikey had been mightily impressed by the cooking pot and said his wife Rose, who runs a West Indian catering business in Tottenham, would love one. So, for a few leones, he bought a brand spanking new pot made from all the recycled rubbish. It wasn't easy getting it back to London, but we did, and now it's doing good service at the Selby Centre in White Hart Lane.

Mikey had been musing about Sierra Leone. He'd noticed that a lot of the people there had similar features to him and were similarly tall. He wondered if perhaps his ancestors had come from there, or whether they were returnees, freed slaves from Jamaica who'd come back.

These questions can never be answered categorically, but on the way back through town we stopped off at the market, which was on the site of the old slave market. I bought a few bits and pieces, including, I'm ashamed to say, a heavy old brass slave ring once used as currency. I later discovered that these were cast in Birmingham, are called manilas, and that one ring would be exchanged for one slave. History can teach us some terrible things. Mikey held up the ring poignantly and said, 'It's history, Major, and you like history, so take it.' The guy at the market stall said that at the back of the market building, the old slave steps leading down to the harbour were still there. We walked round, and Mikey stood on the steps, looked out across the estuary, and muttered to himself, 'I wonder?'

The work finished at Calaba Town with sixteen coaches trained up and the largest number of kids introduced to cricket from any of the trips — over 300 in all. While the disabled had been the priority, one couldn't ignore the clamour from the schools surrounding the quad. We talked to the teachers, who knew a bit about cricket because they were linked to schools in Hull (a nice historical connection, forged because William Wilberforce, the great early 19th-century anti-slaver, came from Hull). The teachers had been watching too, so they'd also learnt about the game and were keen for the kids to continue playing.

One of the ongoing problems in introducing cricket to either poor or non-cricketing countries is getting enough kit to play with, but Francis had found a brilliant solution. His disabled Conforti manufacturing team would make bats and stumps from found materials, so that only balls would be needed — and they're the cheapest and least bulky items anyway. Necessity is the mother of invention, as the old saying goes.

Michael, a teacher and the captain of the Sierra Leone cricket team, had been the most enthusiastic coach all week. Nevertheless he left us with a warning. 'You've been brilliant,' he said. 'But we'll see how good you really are at the match on Saturday.'

The second part of the work was at the Milton Margai School for the Blind. It was tucked away in the backstreets of Freetown, but was a haven of peace for the children there. The headmistress was a Geordie lady called Barbara Davidson who'd devoted her life to the school. Sadly blindness features strongly across the whole of sub-Saharan Africa, but is particularly prevalent in Sierra Leone through river blindness. This is caught from a fly and can be treated fairly easily, but only when the drugs are available, which they rarely are. Similarly, cataracts are common, and again rarely treated because of lack of resources. I read the obituary of a Sierra Leonean the other day, Dr Dennis Williams, who for most of his working career had been the only qualified ophthalmologist in the country. He was reckoned to have led projects that treated nearly a million people suffering from eye problems.

Barbara had heard all about our cricketing mission from the media coverage we'd got, and couldn't wait to see what this blind cricket thing was all about. The children were brought out into the playground, and a demonstration game was set up. None of them had ever played sport before, so the excitement level was at fever pitch. They soon got the hang of it. We could only spend a morning at the school, but that was enough to get the game cemented in their minds, and we left a big bag of kit for them to continue playing.

As a thank you, Barbara got the school choir to sing some songs for us. A few years previously the choir had been to England, where most of the funding for the school comes from, and had produced a wonderful CD, called *Songs from Salone*. One of them is half in English and half in Krio, the Creoles' language, and is called 'Fine Boy, Fine Girl, Fayn Boy, Fayn Gel'. They sing it to help them learn English. Another song, which finished their set, celebrated the end of the civil war, with the tear-jerking lyrics, 'No more guns, no more killing, no more pain, no more killing in the rain, peace.' If ever I'm feeling sorry for myself, I play the haunting Salone CD, and soon realise how good my life is.

Later that day we met Peter Penfold, who happened to be in town. He part-funds the school, and had been British High Commissioner in the early years of the civil war. In 1997 he and his staff had been forced to flee to neighbouring Guinea-Conakry, with the legitimate Sierra Leone government of President Kabbah, when the RUF forces first started to attack Freetown. From a base in Conakry, he stayed on to help the government fight the rebels, and in doing so got involved in an arms deal, 'The Sandline Affair', which was big news at the time. Technically he had breached a UN arms embargo, and having originally been praised for his bravery by Tony Blair was subsequently hung out to dry by our leaders. His contribution to the final peace in Sierra Leone cannot be overestimated and nor can his help for the blind children of Freetown. The Sierra Leoneans certainly appreciate that, for when he finally returned to Freetown in 2002 he was carried shoulder high though the streets on a throne and made a paramount chief.

The hard work over, the local media machine started whirring again, and we were big news in the *Salone Times*, 'The newspaper you can trust', under the banner headline: 'The blind and disabled now play cricket.' Admittedly not that snappy, but certainly accurate.

The media had also highlighted our upcoming cricket match, which was billed as a pipe opener to the Sierra Leone cricket season. First there would be a fifteen-over-a-side ladies match followed by the President's XI (our friend Beresford) versus an England XI, which was surely us.

I was intrigued to see the name of the ground, which was the King Tom ground. Now I don't have many cricket grounds named after me, but I assumed that the name must have recently been assigned to the ground as a mark of respect to me. But no, Beresford told me that King Tom was the name of the local chieftain who first sold land to the British to found Freetown. I still like the name though.

The ground was a wide expanse of red earth surrounded by a stone wall that had been breached many times, and the magnificent cotton wood trees, which must have dated back to King Tom's time. Government forces had been based there during the civil war, so the pavilion had seen better days – a bit like the sad municipal ones you now see in England. But there was a covered stand, and all the disabled players we'd worked with at Calaba Town had been bussed in by Francis to support us, rather than the President's XI, which was touching.

Our team, like a lot of cricket teams, didn't look too bad on paper. A couple of the army guys had come down from Leicester Square, as had a couple of chaps from the High Commission. We also had two of the Sierra Leonean coaches who hadn't been selected for the President's XI, and were thus miffed and raring to go. Mikey skippered our team. He promptly lost the toss, and Michael decided to bat because he said he was 'feeling very confident'. So were we.

But, as Emperor Hirohito said after the bomb fell at Nagasaki, 'Events did not go as well as expected.' Soon the

President's XI raced to 201 for three in their allotted overs, with the added ignominy of their top-scoring batsman, Luseni Senesie, being retired on 59. No excuses, really — their batting was better than our bowling, and our fielding was pretty grim too. Chasing the ball to all four corners of the bumpy outfield in the searing heat, having spent every evening in Paddy's Bar until the early hours was certainly not a situation designed to bring out our best, although the fact that Mikey declined my offer to bowl could also have had an effect, of course.

I tried to hide in the outfield under the shade of one of the cotton wood trees, a ploy which succeeded for a while until a shot rasped past me through a gap in the boundary wall. It finished up in the Commonwealth War Graves cemetery next door, which commemorated the dead, mainly at sea, in two world wars. This gave me some respite from the heat, albeit sad, until I was persuaded to rejoin the game, much-scuffed ball in hand.

Nevertheless, 201 in twenty overs was 'still gettable', said Mikey. 'That's only ten an over,' he added, demonstrating surprising mathematical accuracy. This typical captain's optimism was soon dispelled as we were bowled out for 106 in fifteen overs, a truly dreadful performance. Only Tony batted properly, with a stylish 27, a performance which pleased our disabled friends, who were reassured that at least one of us could play. I came in at number 11 and was not out 0, which for me was quite a decent performance. Michael, the oppo skipper, was delighted as it showed that his players were ready for the oncoming season, and that if they could defeat their old colonial masters, they could probably defeat anyone.

Not getting a bowl and scoring no runs persuaded me that perhaps my playing days were over, and it seemed somehow right that I should declare this at my own ground, the King Tom. At the end of the game I presented all my kit to Michael and, with a tear in my eye, waved farewell to a cricketing career which had lasted over 50 years, and which, while undistinguished, had taken me to some extraordinary places.

I was shaken out of my moment of self indulgence by Beresford, who called everyone to order and proceeded to make a speech thanking us for our work and for providing good opposition for his President's XI. Of course he didn't mean the second part, but it was nice of him to say it, anyway. He then presented me with a framed poster that said 'Certificate of Appreciation for the Outstanding Contribution Made to the Game of Cricket in Sierra Leone'. Luckily, the certificate had been prepared before our match, otherwise it might well have said something different.

We departed from King Tom with great sadness but with some pride. Sierra Leone was rebuilding itself and there were some marvellous people there helping that rebuilding process. David insisted that we should see some of what Sierra Leone used to be like, a land not just of iron and diamonds, but also of beautiful beaches where the famous Bounty commercials used to be shot. We spent a few hours on Lakka beach, and then took a typically painted long narrow boat with an outboard to Beach No. 1, strangely named but even more beautiful than Lakka.

The boat was strangely named too. It was called 'Journey without Maps'.

CONCLUSION
THE THIRD UMPIRE

The third umpire is the one who reviews what's been happening on the pitch from afar, as opposed to me – third man on the pitch. However, putting myself in the third umpire's shoes seems a good way to review the power of cricket to do more than just entertain.

To say that it's been an incredible journey for me doesn't do it justice, especially as that phrase has now been appropriated by Z-list celebrities on reality TV shows. This particular voyage began at home and, to use another well-known expression, charity begins at home. It was the experience we had of helping people in London all those years ago that led to my being able to travel the world, having the most incredible time and hopefully doing some good. I don't feel ashamed to admit that I have had a good time, because all sport is about fun, or should be, and if a sense of personal enjoyment doesn't shine through to the people you're working with, then it's unlikely that the work will succeed.

My own cricketing journey started in Leicester, being dragged somewhat unwillingly down to Grace Road. But in no time I was smitten with the game, just as much as my parents and brother were. Once the bug bites you never seem to be free of it. Ever since, I have found myself searching for the county scores while abroad on holiday and surreptitiously checking the Test score while at work, something

Sir John Major famously used to do in cabinet meetings. I maybe took it a bit too far by playing cricket on my honeymoon in Corfu, but I read that Sir Arthur Conan Doyle, who played first-class cricket and whose only wicket was that of W. G. Grace, was worse than me – apparently he didn't even take his wife on his/their honeymoon!

There is so much to remember from all the countries we visited – the passion of Cuba, the exuberance of Jamaica, the efficiency of New York, the optimism of Rwanda, the thrill of the Nile, the shock of the Victoria Falls and the sheer love of the game in Sri Lanka, are all unforgettable in their different ways. Some of the experiences along the way were not so enjoyable, and even made me wonder whether to carry on. But in such adverse times one is reminded of Israel, where brilliant local people are really trying to bridge the divide between Arab and Jew, and Sri Lanka wracked by bloody civil war, now slowly climbing out of poverty and violence. In both countries cricket is now playing a positive role.

But in the end, it all comes back to home, and what started as a simple love of the game has led me into twenty years of life-changing experiences. Some of the things we've done that have been outlined in this book might be difficult to replicate, but most aren't. If reading this book has opened your eyes to the possibility of helping others with the game, or even just piqued your curiosity, then I have this to say: just go out and try it.

Every cricket club needs volunteers to do all the jobs that we take for granted. Umpires, scorers, coaches, captains, sponsors, drivers, accountants, tea ladies (or gentlemen), event organisers, press liaisons and groundsmen – these are just a few of the roles that any club needs filling. And I know I'll have missed out lots of others. If time is short, it might be a question of simply donating cash instead, as this is always needed, so long as you know where it's going and how it will be used.

Then there's the world of cricket charities, some of which are mentioned in the book. Charities always need volunteers, and indeed staff, too. I'm now proud to be chairman of the Lord's Taverners, the official charity of recreational cricket. Most of its work is in the UK but we've just sent a load of cricket kit out to Jamaica to help Courtney's foundation and I've recently travelled with them to Dubai to raise money there for kids in special needs schools, so the journey continues. The Taverners have spent over 60 years using sport, especially cricket, of course, 'to help give the disadvantaged, especially those with a disability, a sporting chance'. Of course I'm now biased in their favour, but if you look at the back of *Wisden* − and I'm afraid in the 2011 edition you have to go all the way to page 1623 to find it − there's a long list of cricket charities, all of whom I guarantee will want all sorts of help to enable them to achieve their various charitable goals.

Finally there's the route that led to my involvement in using cricket to do good: the jolly cricket tour. When I took a team to India, doing good was the last thing on my mind; we were there to have a good time and maybe play some half-decent cricket. But seeing the pleasure that a couple of our bags of old cricket kit gave to local kids prompted a thought, and a direct approach from one of my players sealed it. So I'd urge anyone who's still playing to find a bunch of other players who fancy a trip abroad. It needn't cost a fortune. It needn't take too long. But it might just lead to something extraordinary, as it did with me.

From time to time cricket, like all sports, suffers from criticism, sometimes deserved, sometimes not. But my experience of the power of the game to do good means that I have retained my optimism and love for it, whatever setbacks it may occasionally face. So for me, the third umpire's decision is a firm 'not out'.

I hope that this book has informed and entertained, but above all I hope that it's enthused at least some readers to pass on their love of the game to others, to use their talents to do good, and hopefully to have as much fun as I've had, on my cricketing 'Journey with Maps'.

INDEX

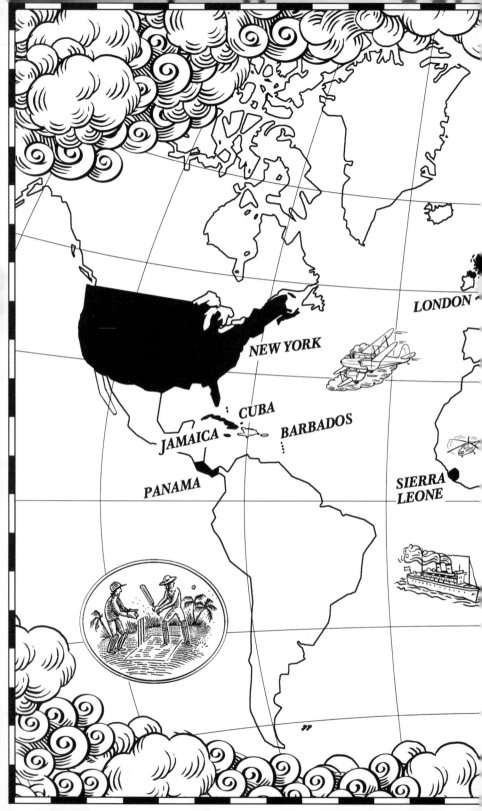

LONDON

NEW YORK

CUBA

JAMAICA

BARBADOS

PANAMA

SIERRA
LEONE